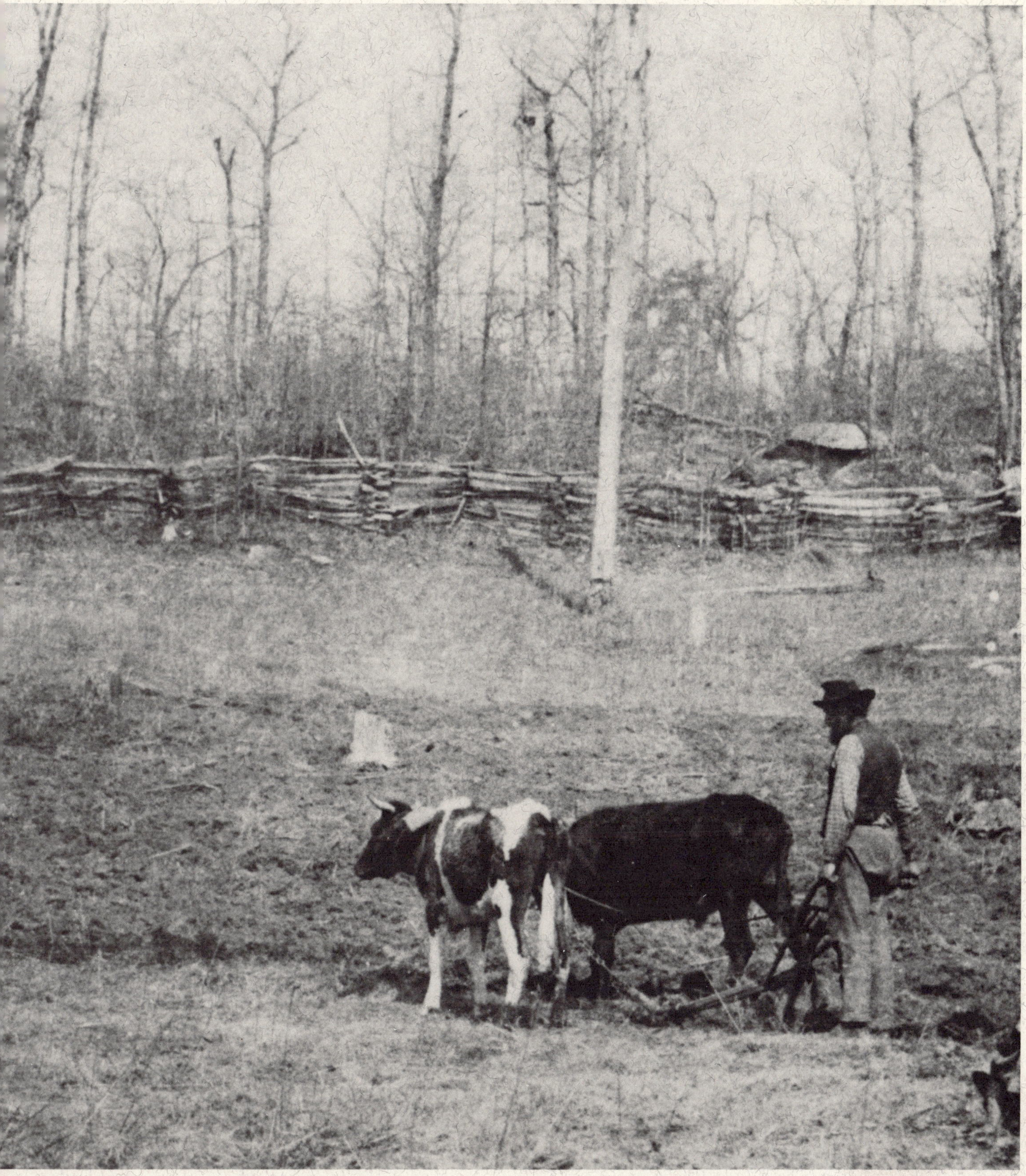

The Buncombe County Board of Commissioners

are very happy to be sponsoring this commemoration of the

county's bicentennial. Commissioners Giezentanner, Sobol, Ledbetter and

Stanley join me in this proud moment in our history.

Gene Rainey
Gene Rainey
Chairman

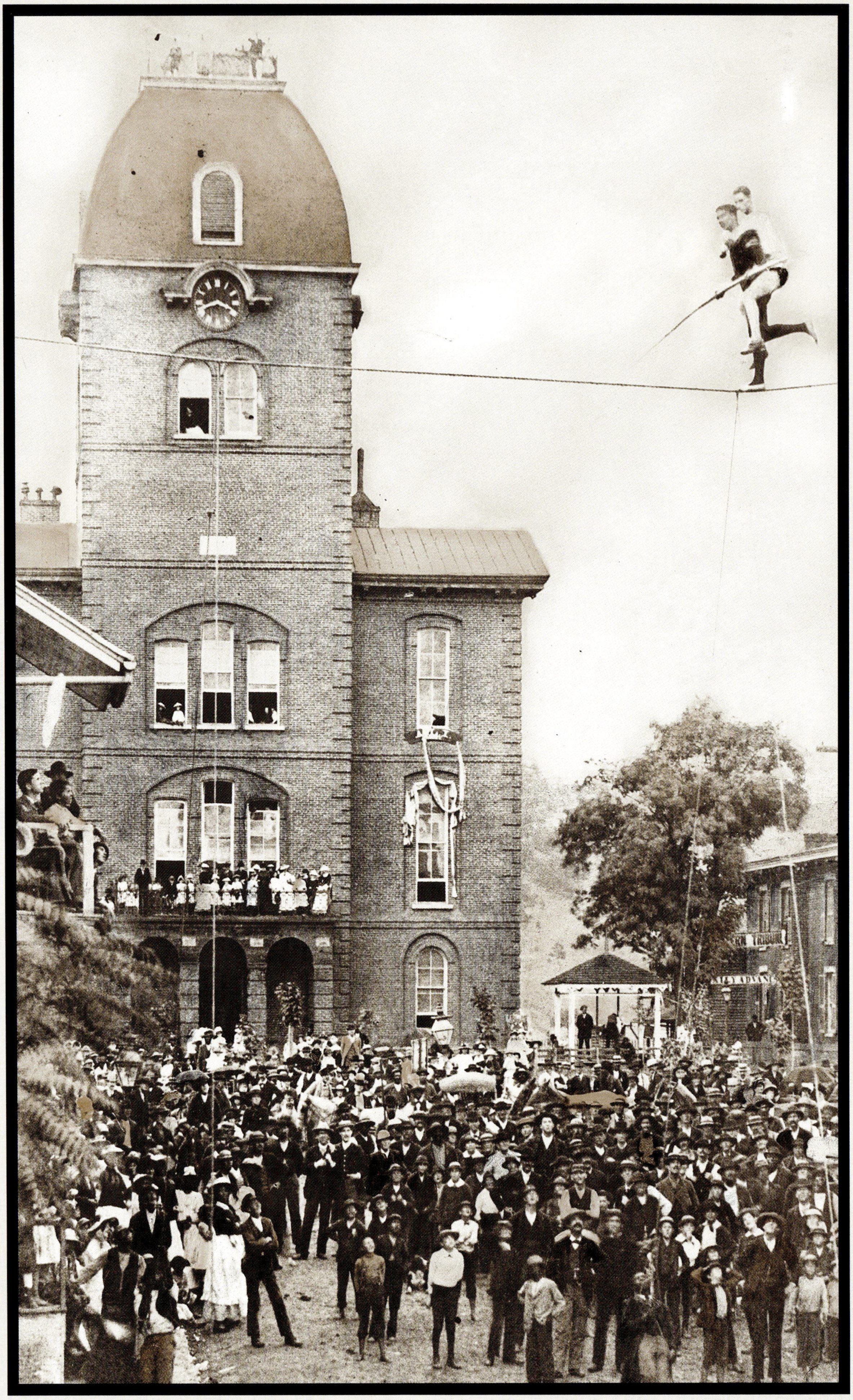

The State of Buncombe

by
Mitzi Schaden Tessier

**THE
DONNING COMPANY**
PUBLISHERS

Endsheets:
Cultivating a plot of ground in mountain soil was often a project for the whole family. The main implement was a crude tool called a "bull-tongue plow," usually made entirely of wood with a small metal point. As a rule farmers followed a method of crop rotation, planting corn one year, rye or wheat the next, and leaving the field fallow the third. Plowing was with the contour of the land. For drainage areas they built check dams or piled brush in the gullies. Because stock ran wild and fed on the woodlands, cleared land and roadways were fenced. Most common was a split-rail fence, which ran zig-zag along the field. In this old picture stumps are still in the field. It often took six years for the roots to rot enough to be removed. Photograph from the North Carolina Collection, Pack Memorial Public Library.

Copyright © 1992 by Mitzi Schaden Tessier

All rights reserved, including the right to reproduce this work in any form whatsoever without permission in writing from the publisher, except for brief passages in connection with a review.
For information, write:
    The Donning Company/Publishers
    184 Business Park Drive, Suite 106
    Virginia Beach, VA 23462

Elizabeth B. Bobbitt, Editor and Coordinator
Richard A. Horwege, Senior Editor
L. J. Wiley, Art Director and Designer
B. L. Walton, Jr., Project Director

Library of Congress Cataloging in Publication Data:

Tessier, Mitzi Schaden, 1924–
    The state of Buncombe/by Mitzi Schaden Tessier.
        p.   cm.
        Includes bibliographical references (p.) and index.
        ISBN 0-89865-832-2 (alk. paper). —ISBN 0-89865-833-0 (pbk. :alk. paper)
        1. Buncombe County (N.C.)—History—Pictorial works. 2. Buncombe County (N.C.)—Description and travel—Views. I. Title.
F262.B94T47   1992
975.6'88—dc20   91-39127
                                                CIP

Printed in the United States of America

Contents

Foreword   7
by Bernard R. Smith

Introduction   9

1776 to 1800   11
The State of Buncombe

1800 to 1830   23
Survival a Way of Life

1830 to 1850   35
Buncombe Meets the World

1850 to 1875   43
A County Divided

1875 to 1890   53
Growth Rode the Rails

1890 to 1900   65
Incorporation Fever

1900 to 1910   81
Men and Money

1910 to 1920   97
Floods, War, and Women's Rights

1920 to 1930   115
Boom and Bust

1930 to 1940   129
Time to Tighten the Belt

1940 to 1960   139
War and Its Aftermath

1960 to 1980   155
Jobs and Roads

1980 to Today   169
Solving Problems for a Bright Tomorrow

Bibliography   189

Index   190

E. E. White worked at Brown's Livery Stable on Sutton Avenue in Black Mountain in 1910. When the horse and buggy was the primary means of transportation, the livery stable was of prime importance to any town's economy. Brown's building burned in 1912 in a disastrous Black Mountain fire that started in J. I. Bradham's Livery Stable on Cherry Street. There was no central water system in the town, so the citizens set up a bucket brigade from their wells to fight the fire. Photograph courtesy of the Valley Museum, Black Mountain.

Foreword

On January 14, 1992, Buncombe County will celebrate the two-hundreth anniversary of its birth as a county of the State of North Carolina.

In 1791, a petition presented to the North Carolina House of Commons by Col. David Vance and Col. William Davidson was passed. The following year the bill was ratified, creating Buncombe County from a division of Burke and Rutherford counties.

Vance lived in the upper Reems Creek area and Davidson's home was at Gum Spring, near the site of the present entrance to Biltmore Estate.

The new county was named for Col. Edward Buncombe, a North Carolina officer who was wounded at the Battle of Germantown and later died while a prisoner of the British.

It is of more than passing interest that Edward Buncombe, according to historian Foster A. Sondley, lived for about ten years in Tyrell County, North Carolina, on land bequeathed to him by an uncle, Joseph Buncombe, and on whose land Edward erected a large home known as Buncombe Hall.

Buncombe County has thrived in the past two centuries, some years better than others, but on balance, a period that has seen Buncombe grow from an essentially agrarian economy to an economy fueled by diverse interests — agriculture, business, industry, and perhaps the most important of all, tourism, as evidenced by the thousands of visitors who enter our county each year.

In this volume on Buncombe County, author Mitzi Tessier has produced a worthy sequel to her earlier historical volume, Asheville: A Pictorial History.

This book features three hundred historical photographs and a text capturing the past two centuries of life in Buncombe County.

Sponsored by the County of Buncombe, this new pictorial history is a most valuable contribution to the 1992 events planned by the Buncombe County Bicentennial Commission honoring the two-hundredth anniversary of our county.

Bernard R. Smith
Chairman, Buncombe County
Bicentennial Commission

Asheville's Rhododendron Festival provided a happy release for people from 1928 to 1942. They crowded the city to see the many parades and other activities. In the baby parade of the 1939 festival Cinderella and her court won a silver loving cup. The float, shown here beside the Grove Arcade before the windows were bricked up, was made over a wagon by the children's father Paul Pless. In the parade are the Plesses, Rose Mary as Cinderella; Margaret, fairy godmother, and Joe, Prince Charming. Pulling the float were Martha Pless and Rose Shore. Photograph courtesy of Rose Case.

Introduction

A man who never lived in the county created a legacy for Buncombe County. It happened in 1817 in the Fifteenth Congress.

All day the legislators had labored over a bill concerning pensions for the states' militia. When the call for adjournment came, Felix Walker rose to his feet and demanded that he be allowed five minutes "to speak for Buncombe." Since that day "speaking for Buncombe" has been applied to those who waste time with useless talk. The word "bunk" derives from "Buncombe."

Despite the legend, however, Buncombe is not a lot of bunk. The devotion given by so many to keeping the county's history is strong evidence of that point. Their enthusiasm and interest made writing this book a pleasure.

Buncombe's book is different from our other pictorial album *Asheville: A Pictorial History*. It's not the story of the rich and famous. It's the story of stalwart, hardworking people, who, in spite of a simple environment, have used their intelligence to maintain Buncombe's position as a regional leader. Used with *Asheville*, this book will give the reader a broader perspective of Buncombe and its county seat, the City of Asheville.

Names of individuals whose pictures I have used are under the pictures. In addition, I would like to thank the keepers of special collections, the North Carolina Collection at Pack Memorial Library, Southern Highlands Research Center at the University of North Carolina at Asheville, Valley Museum in Black Mountain, Dry Ridge Museum in Weaverville, Smith-McDowell House, and Southern Highland Handicraft Guild. Also, thanks to Larry White for photographic reproduction.

The book itself is a tribute to these and others who shared knowledge, slides, and encouragement. If I were to make a dedication, it would be to them and my long-suffering family.

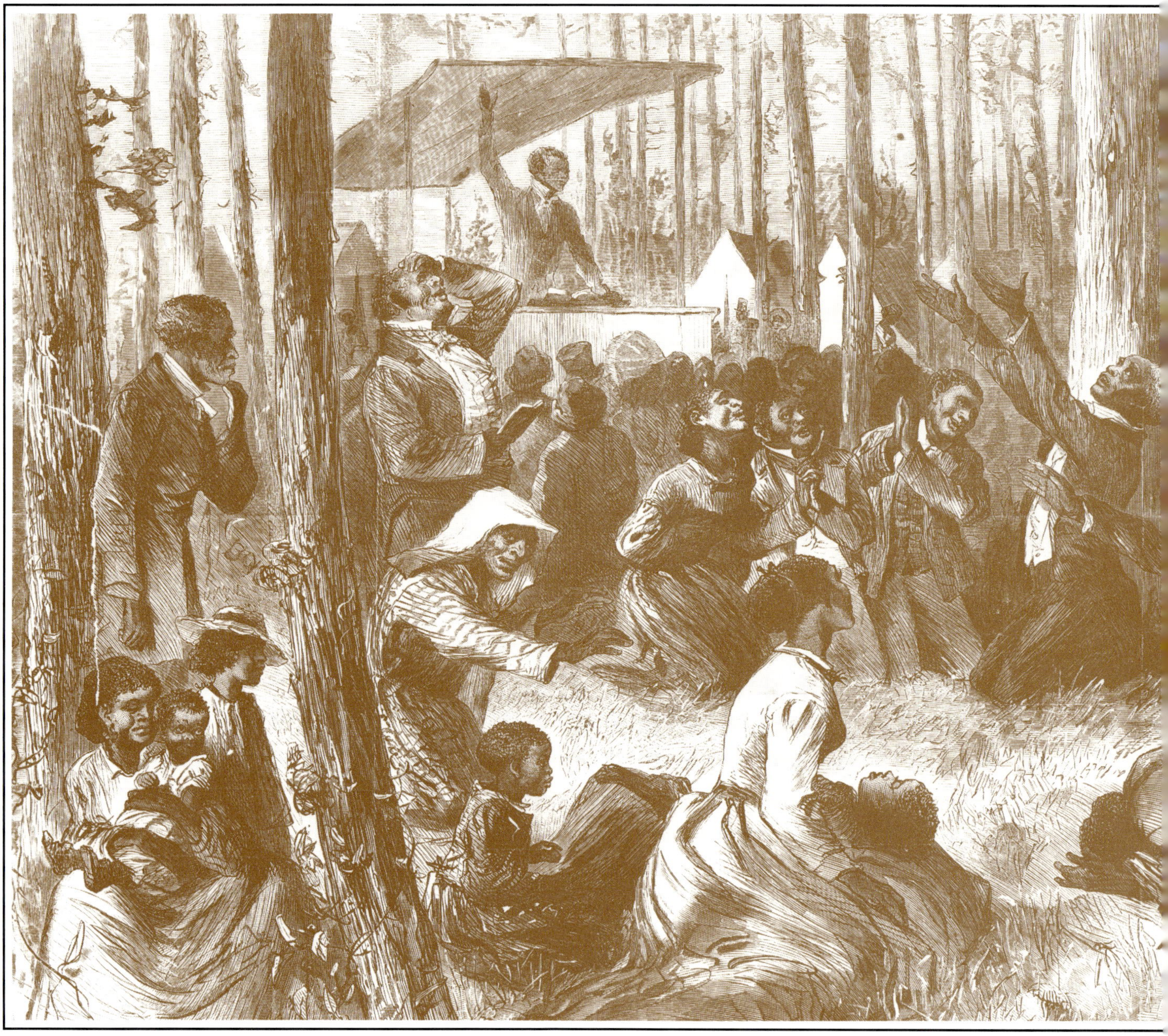

The State of Buncombe
1776 to 1800

What really happened behind the veil of the blue mountains remains a Revolutionary War mystery. Did Captain William Hamilton Moore, Indian fighter, patriot, husband, father, and early settler of Buncombe County build a fort at Hominy Creek and remain in it periodically from 1776 to 1784? Or did Moore return to his home on Muddy Creek near Dysartsville after his 1776 expeditions against the Cherokees?

Few facts are available. Military records show that Moore passed through the Swannanoa Gap in September 1776 with Brigade General Griffith Rutherford and twenty-five hundred members of the North Carolina State Militia bound for the western villages of the Cherokees. Their mission was to erase the Indian threat, to free the settlers east of the mountains from the enemy who had raided their farms and killed their people.

Rutherford's men burned villages and crops but killed few Indians. A few months later Captain Moore returned with a smaller brigade of lighthorsemen and rode as far west as the Tuckaseegee River. They destroyed two more Indian towns but the enemy remained at large.

An emergency meeting was called in 1777 in Salisbury. Moore and Rutherford attended, as well as Indian fighter John Sevier of the Watauga settlement and other civil authorities and military men. An unpublished manuscript believed to have been written by Judge Owen Gudger, county historian who grew up in Hominy Valley, says Moore left for the western lands following that meeting.

With Moore was a small army, enough men to defend a fort and keep the Indians from moving east to join the British. To strengthen the defense, the army erected blockhouses in four directions from Hominy: east toward the gap in the Alleghenies, now called Swannanoa; south along the Watauga or Bear Creek Trail to South Carolina; north to the Bear Creek Ford where the trail crossed the French Broad in what is now Madison County, and west to the present Haywood line. Each blockhouse was a bugle call

Facing page:
Camp meetings were a popular way for people to gather on the frontier. Families would fill their wagons with provisions for the week and travel to Salem, Turkey Creek, Newfound, Sand Hill, Edneyville, or other locations to hear the preaching and socialize. Harry Hozier, known as "Black Harry" was a popular preacher on the camp meeting circuit. He traveled with Bishop Francis Asbury into Buncombe County on several trips and preached at camp meetings, love feasts, and quarterly sessions. He was praised by fellow churchmen as "the greatest orator of his day." One said, "Harry was a more popular speaker than Asbury." Most of the camp meetings continued until the 1850s when more congregations began to build churches. Ben Lippen school and Eliada Home for Children, however, sponsored something of the same nature until the 1970s. Engraving from the Library of Congress Collection.

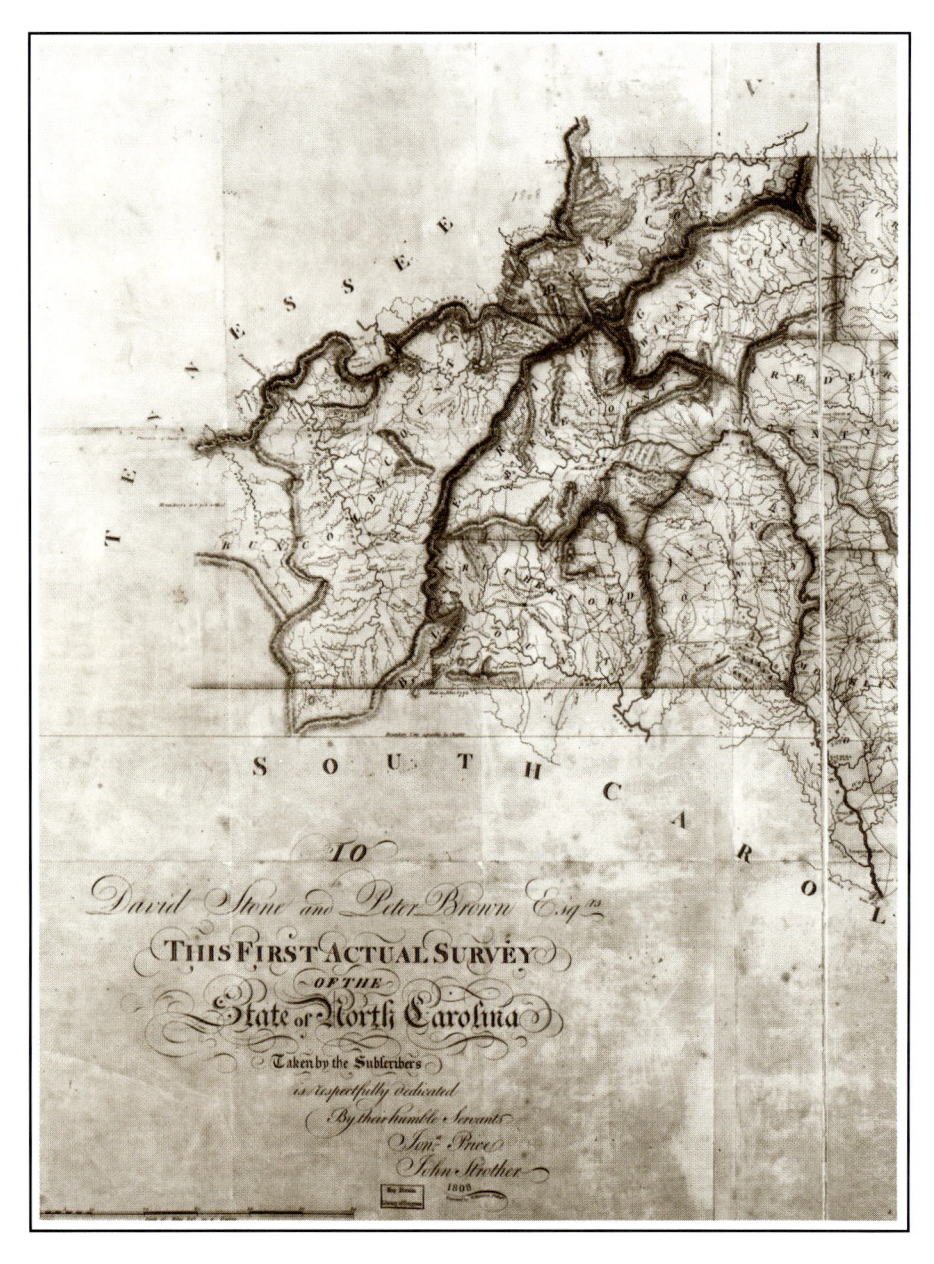

The first survey map of the state of North Carolina was drawn by Jonathan Price and John Strother and issued in 1808. The western section of the map shows in detail the rivers and creeks, some residences, and early roads. The extent of the "State of Buncombe" had not been determined when the map was drawn, so the surveyors indicated "borders not settled" to the west. Haywood County, established in 1809, is not marked; however, its borders followed the range of mountains west of the French Broad River. Asheville is written as "Morristown." John Strother, a resident of Buncombe, was one of two surveyors who ran the line for the Tennessee-North Carolina border. He also acted as an agent for John Gray Blount of Beaufort County, one of the men who owned over a million acres of land in Buncombe County. Map courtesy of the Library of Congress.

away from the next one, a bugle being an ox or cow horn.

Among the men stationed on this western frontier were William Cannon at Tan Yard Branch; Rogers, Lance, Case, and Abraham Reynolds at Bent Creek; two Warrens and one Davis at South Hominy; Thompson at Thompson's Knob, and Bill MacFee.

North of the fort were James Rutherford, John George, William Penland, Moore's sons Thomas and William, Jr., Gabriel Ragsdale, Dryman, and Spivey.

The manuscript says that Moore built a stockade around the fort and a rock house for his own use. In addition, several log houses and a guest house were in the compound to take care of travelers on the Bear Creek Trail.

The western lands baffled North Carolina after the Revolutionary War. In 1763 King George had decreed that land west of the Blue Ridge be set aside for the Cherokees. Because he had prohibited entry into, or grant of, that land, it was unsettled. After the Treaty of Paris in 1783 the land belonged to the sovereign state of North Carolina, but Carolina owed a huge war dept to the Continental Congress.

To escape the debt, the General Assembly in the spring of 1784 voted to cede the lands west of the mountains to the federal government. Before Congress had time to act, however, the Assembly repealed the vote and began offering land grants for sale in western lands.

Earliest land grants recorded for what would become Buncombe County were issued August 7, 1787, for Captain Moore, Col. William Davidson, and his brother James Davidson. Moore's grant included the War ford on the French Broad and choice land along Hominy Creek. The Davidson grant was on the Swannanoa River, near its conflux with the French Broad.

Population in 1791 from the Blue Ridge west was estimated at one thousand, not including Indians. This estimate, based on the first U.S. census of 1790, included all the western counties now within the boundaries of the State of North Carolina.

In the fall of 1791 Col. David Vance and Col. William Davidson rode to New Bern with petitions asking the General Assembly to divide Burke and Rutherford counties and form a new county of the western territories. This county was to be called Union. When the bill was ratified on January 14, 1792, Union County was named Buncombe for Col. Edward Buncombe, Revolutionary War hero from North Carolina.

Territory gained by the new county was unexplored Indian territory. It was known to be so vast that many referred to it as the "State of Buncombe."

The tiny county seat was rough. John Brown, who rode his horse from Philadelphia to Morristown, as Asheville was known in 1795, wrote in his diary that the town was a collection of rude log huts (one of which was the courthouse), with so much vermin and lice that he and his partner preferred to sleep out.

The movement of people into the area improved the ancient Indian trails and made them wagon roads. About the time Brown wrote his diary, Zebulon and Bedent Baird brought a wagonload of goods into the county and opened a store. By January 27, 1798, when the commissioners for Asheville took office, the village had begun to take shape.

At a spot known as Gum Springs, just inside the gates of the Biltmore Estate, the first meeting of the Buncombe County Court of Pleas and Quarterly Session was called on April 16, 1792. This was the home of Col. William Davidson. When the interested people had arrived, the crowd was too large for the house, so court convened in Davidson's barn, which was located on the side of a hill about one hundred yards southwest of his residence, according to Dr. Foster Sondley in his History of Buncombe County. Early maps show the road running parallel to the Swannanoa River on the south side where the entry road to the Biltmore Estate is now located. The block work around Gum Springs was placed there when the Estate was built in the early 1890s, so water from the spring could be pumped to the gate house. Photograph by Jack Tessier.

Abraham Reynolds began acquiring state grants for land at Bent Creek in 1800. He received seven grants which totaled 1,525 acres. He and his wife, Mary Leazer Reynolds, built a log cabin on his property and lived there with his family of twelve children. This picture of the cabin was made in the 1920s when Boy Scout Executive A. W. Allen lived there with his family. Allen was developing the first Camp Daniel Boone which was on Bent Creek property. Photograph courtesy of Thomas Reynolds.

Blockhouses that surrounded Hominy Valley and extended up and down the French Broad to protect the settlements from the Cherokees were described as two-story log buildings with portholes big enough for muskets. This building was photographed in 1989 on the grounds of the James Gudger house on Turkey Creek, the first portion of which was built in 1805. Photograph courtesy of Eleanor N. Rice.

Commerce in the small county seat included the sale of firewood and fence posts. Revealed in this early photo of a location near Public Square are several modes of transportation. A small store on the left is open for trade. The shed in the background may have been a public market or a livery stable. Photograph from the North Carolina Collection, Pack Memorial Library.

Colonel David Vance and his wife Pricilla Brank Vance built a two-story log house at Vanceville on Reems Creek sometime before 1790. At the time Vance was the representative from Burke County in the North Carolina House of Commons. He immediately became prominent in the western territory, for in 1791 he and Col. William Davidson, who represented Rutherford County, carried petitions from the people to the General Assembly in New Bern asking that a new county be formed west of the mountains. Vance was elected clerk at the first Buncombe County Court of Pleas, April 16, 1792, and served in this office for many sessions. In 1799 Vance joined Gen. Joseph McDowell and Mussendine Matthews as North Carolina commissioners to supervise the placement of the Tennessee border from Virginia to the Cataloochee trail. Many of Vance's children and grandchildren were born under this roof, including Gen. R. B. Vance of Civil War fame and former governor Zebulon B. Vance. The house has been recreated on the original property and is now open as a State Historic Site. Photograph from the North Carolina Collection, Pack Memorial Public Library.

Samuel Davidson, considered by many historians to be the first settler in Buncombe County, came from the Catawba River Valley in 1784, crossed the Blue Ridge Mountains to Christian Creek near the Swannanoa River, and built a cabin there. Davidson may have gone unnoticed as just another settler but because of his tragic death, his story is documented. Shortly after his arrival in the mountains, Davidson was ambushed by Indians, lured out of his cabin by the sound of his horse's bell. His wife, hearing the sound of a rifle shot, fled with her infant daughter and female slave and sounded the alarm at Davidson's Fort, now Old Fort. Samuel's twin brother William Davidson and their sister Rachael Alexander joined other relatives and formed a colony on Bee Tree Creek. As to the grave, there is a story that Capt. William Moore and his men avenged the killing of Davidson in a battle with the Indians. Photograph from the North Carolina Collection, Pack Memorial Public Library.

Buncombe County was the stopping-off place for early settlers moving west, including Davy Crockett. As his buddy in the Revolutionary War lay dying, he asked Crockett to take his belongings to his wife in North Carolina. Following the war Davy traveled to the Bee Tree settlement, found Elizabeth (Polly) Patton, and carried out his buddy's wishes. Davy left, so the story goes, but his memory of Polly was so strong that he came back for her and took her on to Texas as his wife. The tree pictured here is one that Davy used for target practice while he was in Buncombe County. Davy died a hero in the Alamo and Polly was so loved that Texas erected a statue in her memory at the scene of the battle. Photograph from the North Carolina Collection, Pack Memorial Public Library.

Benjamin Stringfield Brittain, son of James and Delilah Stringfield Brittain, was a pioneer son born in Buncombe County in 1793. As treaties were made with the Indians and counties formed to the west, Brittain left the county and moved to Haywood, Macon, and later Cherokee County. Brittain had been brought up in a political household. His father was a justice of peace on the first Buncombe County Court of Pleas and Quarter Sessions and a member of the commission that decided on the placement of the first Buncombe County Court House. Brittain served as sheriff of Buncombe from 1818 to 1824. He was married to Celia Vance, daughter of Col. David Vance of Reems Creek. She is shown with him, circa 1860. Photograph courtesy of Shirley Brittain Cawyer.

Scotch-Irish settlers brought their religion with them. Within two years of the founding of the county, Presbyterian congregations were meeting at Bee Tree, the Swannanoa settlement, Reems Creek, and Cane Creek. The Reverend George Newton, who came into the county in 1797 as an ordained Presbyterian minister, preached to all four congregations. In addition, he took over teaching duties from Robert Henry at Union Hill School, later to be called Union Academy, later Newton School. Union Hill is said to be the first school west of the Blue Ridge. Newton remained in Buncombe County until 1814, when he moved to Bedford County, Tennessee. E. M. Porter, another Presbyterian teacher-preacher took over his duties. Photograph from the North Carolina Collection, Pack Memorial Public Library.

Rivers to be crossed had to be forded in the days before ferries or bridges. Three main fords existed on the French Broad: Long Shoals where the Long Shoals Road is today; the War ford about two miles above the mouth of the Swannanoa, called by some the Rutherford ford because General Griffith Rutherford chose that route in 1776, and the Bear Creek ford between today's Marshall and Hot Springs in Madison County. In making a crossing, a zig-zag course was often necessary and those not familiar with the river could have difficulty. Steroscopic photograph from the North Carolina Collection, Pack Memorial Public Library.

Progress and development took a landmark before the preservationists could save it. This house in Turkey Creek Community was probably the oldest house in the county, one portion having been built in 1805 by James Gudger and the other portion in 1850 by his son Adolphus. In the late 1980s it and the land around it were bought by a developer. The house was advertised by the Historic Resources Commission for sale if someone would move it. When there were no takers, the preservationists tried to give it to someone who would preserve it. Finally, in 1989 the house was razed. The Gudgers were an early pioneer family. William Gudger, Sr., was an Indian-fighter who moved to Buncombe County sometime before 1786 and settled on the Swannanoa about where the Buncombe County Golf Course is now. His son James married a daughter of Robert Love. Love, who is commonly associated with Haywood County, owned vast acreage in the northern section of Buncombe County. The Gudgers settled in Turkey Creek, but James Gudger remained active in county politics. He represented Buncombe in the North Carolina State Senate in 1820 and 1836. He owned many slaves and is credited with developing the first strain of corn that would reproduce in mountain soil. Photograph courtesy of Eleanor N. Rice.

A rushing mountain stream was an important power source for the pioneer. Gristmills which ground corn and wheat were located in various sections of the county. To protect the investment of the miller, the Buncombe County Court of Pleas required that mills be sanctioned by the court. First mills approved were for John Burton on Glenn's Creek, north of the courthouse, and William Davidson, on the Swannanoa River. The mill wheel pictured is turning water from Reems Creek. It may have powered the woolen mill there or the gristmill which came later. Photograph from the North Carolina Collection, Pack Memorial Public Library.

Caroline Lane Swain was the mother of two men whose lives made a difference to history. Col. James Lowry was the son of Caroline and David Lowry. His father was killed by Indians. Colonel Lowry settled in Sandy Mush about 1800 and served in Congress for several terms. David Lowry Swain, born 1801 on Beaverdam Creek to Caroline and George Swain, was governor of North Carolina, from 1832 to 1835, and president of the University of North Carolina at Chapel Hill for thirty years. There is in the family a letter from Caroline Lane Swain written to Lowry when he was in Congress. She told him, "I have no objection to your moving in a public sphere of life provided I knew that the Good of your country and the Will of God called you there....I fear lest Satan gain an advantage by inspiring your mind with a hankering after the fruit of the tree of knowledge." North Carolina ratified the Constitution on November 21, 1789; the letter was written in 1815. How quickly she learned that politics could corrupt a man. Photograph courtesy of Maybre Candler Brenton.

In 1800 Methodist Bishop Francis Asbury began to travel up the French Broad River to "Buncombe Courthouse," Little River, and beyond. In his diary of November 6, 1800, he wrote of the trials of his travel. On that day his roan horse had reeled and fallen over, taking his chaise with it and almost dumping him in the water. Later he "passed the side fords of the French-Broad." Asbury was traveling a road older than the Buncombe Turnpike. This old stereoscopic picture is of a side ford in the river, a necessity when the rocks were too high and steep to build a road. Photograph from the North Carolina Collection, Pack Memorial Public Library.

When Bishop Francis Asbury was a frequent visitor at the home of Daniel Killian, his host made a chair for him. One of Killian's granddaughters, either Miss Josie or Miss Julia, is pictured with the chair on the front porch of a house on Beaverdam Road in which the ladies lived for many years. Beaverdam residents remember the sisters in their caps and dark cloaks, always dressed as they would have been in the early 1800s. According to members of Asbury United Methodist Church, where the chair has been preserved, Killian made the back taller but it was sawed off to make souvenir walking sticks. Photograph courtesy of Asbury United Methodist Church.

The rude log cabin behind these women on washday may have been the family's springhouse. It may have been their home. This was a postcard picture of a mountain family, printed for the trades. It was common, however, well into the 1920s, for washing to be done in a bucket over the fire, rinsed in another tub, and hung to dry. Photograph from the North Carolina Collection, Pack Memorial Public Library.

Survival a Way of Life
1 8 0 0 to 1 8 3 0

Who were these people who populated Buncombe County? Why were they willing to make the personal sacrifices to carve a home out of the wilderness? Estimates vary as to how many were of Scotch, Irish, English, German, French Hugenot, or African origin. The numbers change by community. In the earliest settlements Bee Tree, Swannanoa, and Reems Creek—Scotch-Irish names were predominant.

Those who live in Buncombe today would say the "why" is evident. The climate and beauty of the county attracts settlers. Frontier people, however, were nomads in search of land, independence, and freedom of religion. For the Scotch-Irish, the journey from Scotland had begun a century earlier when their ancestors went to Ireland for the same reasons.

"The State of Buncombe" was divided in 1809 when the General Assembly separated Haywood County. Six counties were later formed of Haywood. In 1833 parts of Burke and Buncombe became Yancey. Buncombe gave up Henderson in 1838. Then, with the formation of Madison from Buncombe and Yancey in 1851, county lines were drawn until 1925 when Buncombe annexed the community known as French Broad.

For all, life on the frontier was a struggle for survival. The Buncombe County slogan, "People to Match the Mountains," is appropriate. It took stalwart men and women to meet the challenge.

Feeling of community was strong in the settlers. The Sawyer community at the head of Reems Creek was photographed in the 1800s. Much of the property owned by early settlers was divided for their children to have homesites. In this way, large farms became smaller until many found themselves without enough land to support their families. A community of this size could be almost self-sufficient, with a blacksmith, gristmill, school, church, and a small store. Photograph courtesy of "Pat" Rhea Hensley.

A cabin built in the Sandy Mush area reflects life as it was on the frontier. Francis Josiah Jones, known as Cy, cut poplar logs from the woods and squared them to build a home. The family remembers that Cy's son Horace was bitten by a copperhead snake while helping his father. To stack the dry-laid chimney Cy gathered field stones. Roof shingles were cut from a chestnut sapling. As in all rural areas of Buncombe until a much later day, the house had no electricity, running water, or bathrooms. Inside was a room for family living and a loft where the children slept. Yet, the view of Dogged Mountain in the distance, fresh water from nearby Sugar Creek, and plenty of land for farming and raising stock helped Cy Jones care for his family. The house was recently taken down, but the logs were saved. The family has hopes that someday the cabin may be rebuilt. Photograph courtesy of James H. Coman.

Fresh water and mountain springs were sought when settlers chose a place for a homesite. This stereoscopic picture of children at a fountain of mountain spring water looks Victorian, but it could have been made in earlier times or even today. Many county people still get their water from the springs that were found and used by their ancestors. Photograph from the North Carolina Collection, Pack Memorial Public Library.

Keeping the hearth fire burning was important to the mountain people, for the fireplace was where family members cooked and warmed themselves. Matches were a luxury, so if the fire went out, it was necessary to get a spark from a flint or go to a neighbor's cabin for fire. Often the fire was carried on a corn shuck, thus the expression "Did you just come to light a shuck?" when a guest doesn't stay long. Details in this old postcard reveal much about pioneer life, such as the man's boots made of deerskin, cornbread in the cast iron pot, papers on the wall for insulation, and handmade furniture. Photograph from the North Carolina Collection, Pack Memorial Public Library.

A homemade sled carried children, tow sacks of corn, kindlin', or a pile of rocks. With a bullock to pull it, a sled could conquer most hilly slopes or rough terrain. Photograph from the North Carolina Collection, Pack Memorial Public Library.

A fall ritual was making "lasses" from sorghum cane. After a horse or mule turned the grinder to extract the sweet juice from the sorghum cane, the juice was boiled over a furnace until it turned into dark, thick molasses, fit to put on biscuits or hot cakes on a winter morning. Many people remember the fun of molasses pulls. Sorghum molasses cooked in a skillet will thicken enough to be worked and pulled to form a creamy candy. Molasses is a plural noun. "The molasses are good." William A. Barnhill photograph from the North Carolina Collection, Pack Memorial Public Library.

Before the state fence law of 1885, stock had the run of the forest to fatten up on mast, acorns, and chestnuts. Each farmer could identify his cows and hogs with a brand cut into an ear. Because it could be preserved well by curing with salt, canning, or smoking, hogs were an important food source in early Buncombe. Today farmers no longer brand stock and let the animals roam, but hog butcherings are common. November, when cold has set in, is the time to butcher. First the hog is slaughtered and properly bled; then, it's dipped in hot water and scraped with something like a dull knife. All parts of the hog are good for eating, the head for souse or hog's head stew, the internal organs for livermush and chitterlings (chitlins), and the feet for pickling. Lean meat pieces are seasoned for sausage and the fat rendered for lard. The house in this picture was in Beech community. Photograph courtesy of "Pat" Rhea Hensley.

Churning was an all day job. Cream strained off the milk had to clabber before it was poured into the old barrel churn. Then women and children took turns working the handle until the "butter came." The family stored butter in the springhouse until they were ready to use it or sell it in town. Photograph by William H. Barnhill from the North Carolina Collection, Pack Memorial Public Library.

Much of the Buncombe Turnpike followed an older road which is known to have existed in 1795. The turnpike extended from Greeneville, Tennessee, to Greenville, South Carolina. The General Assembly chartered the Turnpike Company in 1824 and directed James Patton, Samuel Chunn, and George Swain to receive subscriptions for the purpose of laying out and making a road that would enter Buncombe County at Saluda Gap on the south and exit at Paint Rock, Tennessee. The road opened in 1828. In 1850 the part of this road south of Asheville was covered with planks and called the Greenville to Asheville Plank Road. This stereoscopic picture, one of the few photographs of the turnpike in existence, is from the North Carolina Collection, Pack Memorial Public Library.

Long before there were bridges, ferries operated in several locations along the French Broad River. Capt. Edmund Sams built one in Asheville near the spot where the old Smith Bridge crossed. He sold it to John Jarrett, who sold it to James McConnell Smith. Smith built the bridge. At Craggy, Col. William Gorman operated a ferry until Gorman's Bridge was built. Col. James Mitchell Alexander operated one at Alexander where his inn was. In Madison County Col. Samuel Chunn and Philip Hoodenpile maintained ferries. An artist from Harpers Magazine sketched this scene in 1867. Photograph from the North Carolina Collection, Pack Memorial Public Library.

Fish from the rivers remained a primary food source for mountain people well into the twentieth century. A fish trap placed at the shoal in the river could yield so many fish that large barrels would be required to carry them home. This fish trap is in the Swannanoa River. Photograph from the North Carolina Collection, Pack Memorial Public Library.

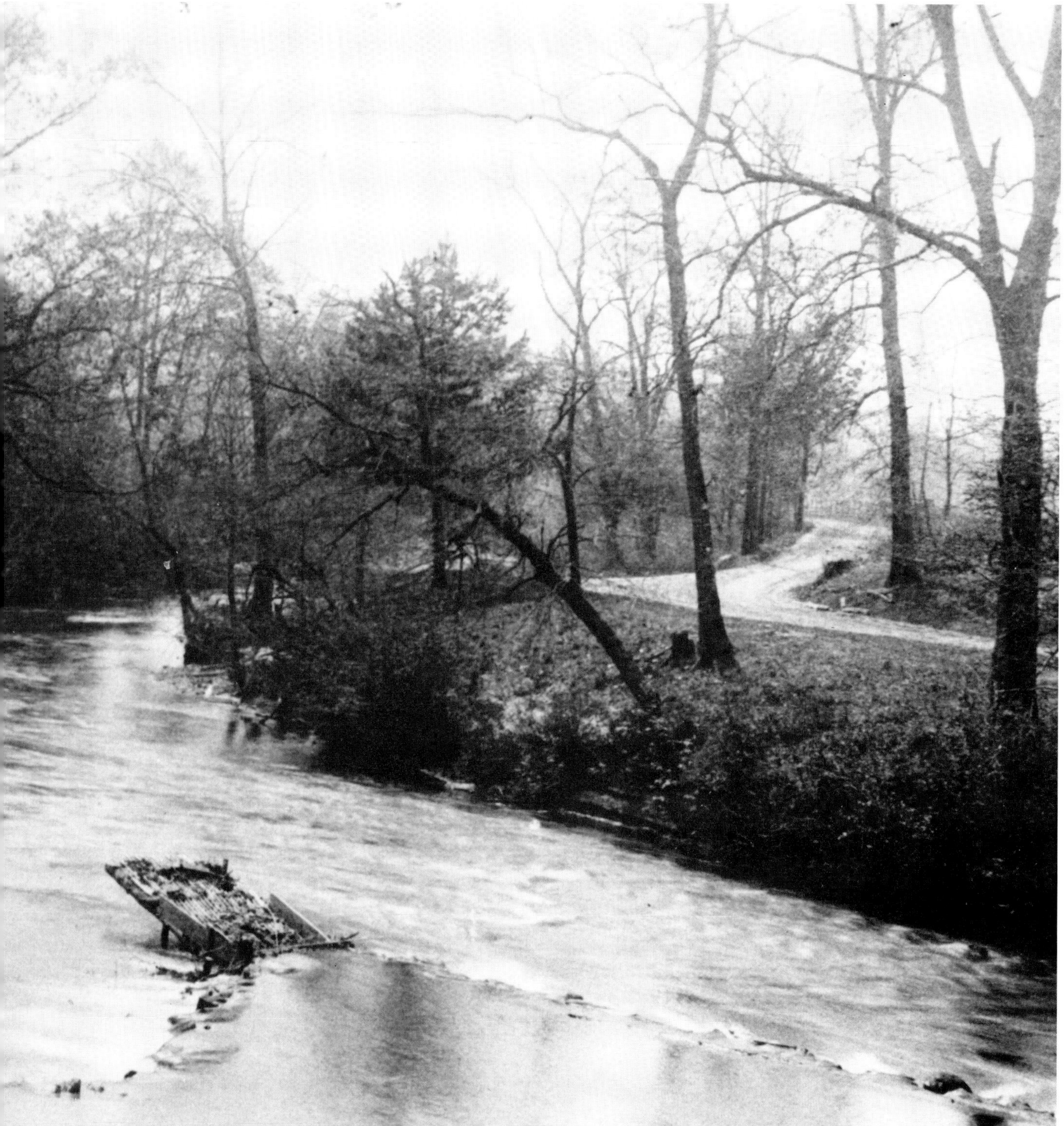

Of this photograph, photographer W. A. Barnhill wrote, "The setting is on the porch of the cabin of the Warrens at Pisgah, North Carolina made in the summer of 1915-16. It shows the complete cycle of using wool from the sheep to make useful articles. The various stages of making a quilt or coverlet goes as follows: 1. wash the wool; 2. turn the wool on a big spinning wheel to make thread, 3. card it by hand, 4. goes on spindle to pull thread out, and 5. prepare loom by weaving thread back and forth for the size and pattern of the coverlet to be woven. Of course, this is a slow tedious procedure. The various members of the family helped with the various tasks. Cindy Warren was the spinner. Her grandmother spun the thread, and other members carded the wool by hand." The Chester Cogburns adopted Cindy and her brother Henry and brought them up on Pisgah View Ranch. Photograph courtesy of Max Cogburn.

Facing page:
Except for a stuffed doll or a hand carved wagon, toys were hard to come by in mountain homes. A piglet or chicken to chase or a pony to ride often took the place of "store bought" playthings. Photograph by William A. Barnhill, from the North Carolina Collection, Pack Memorial Public Library.

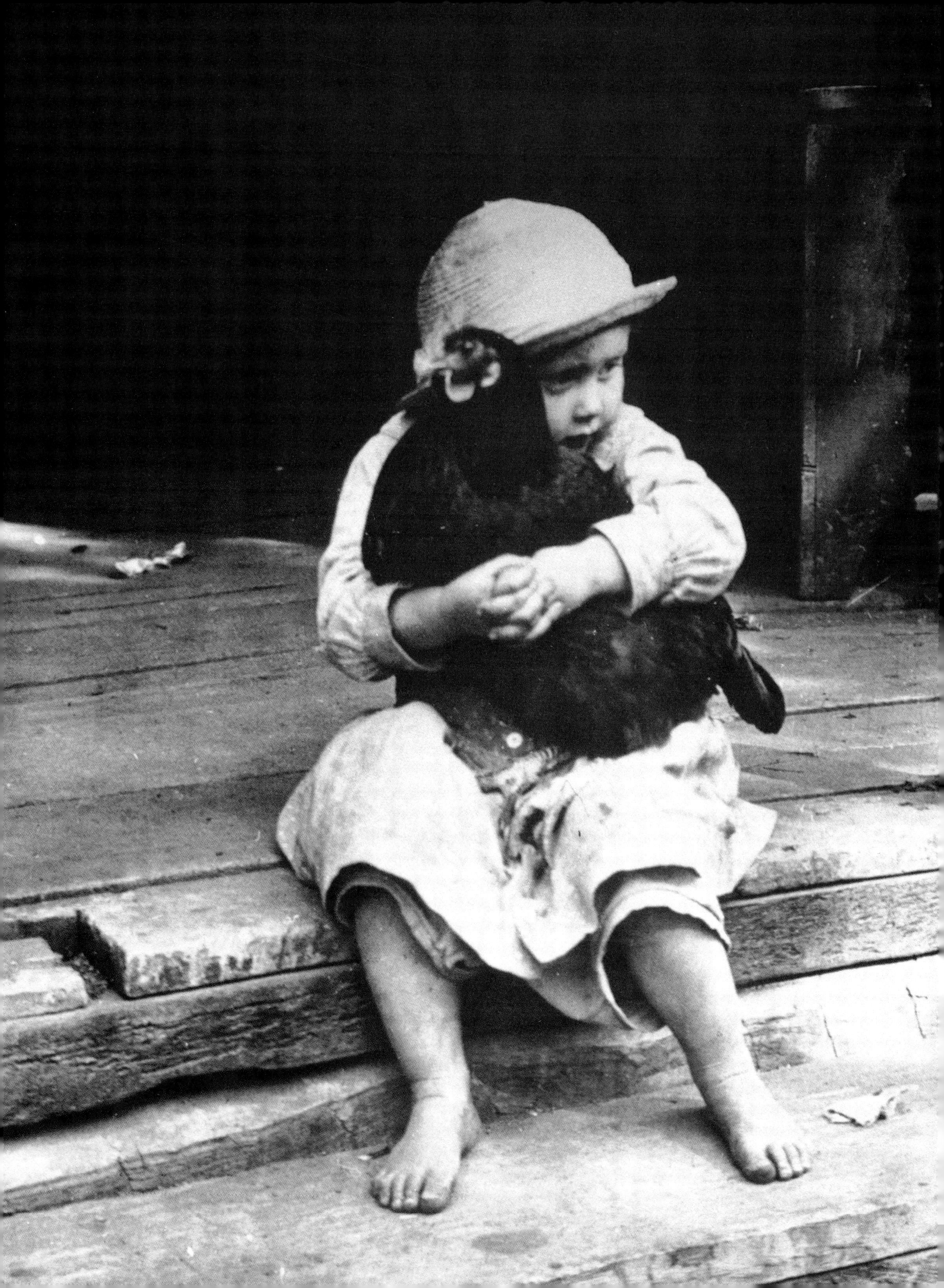

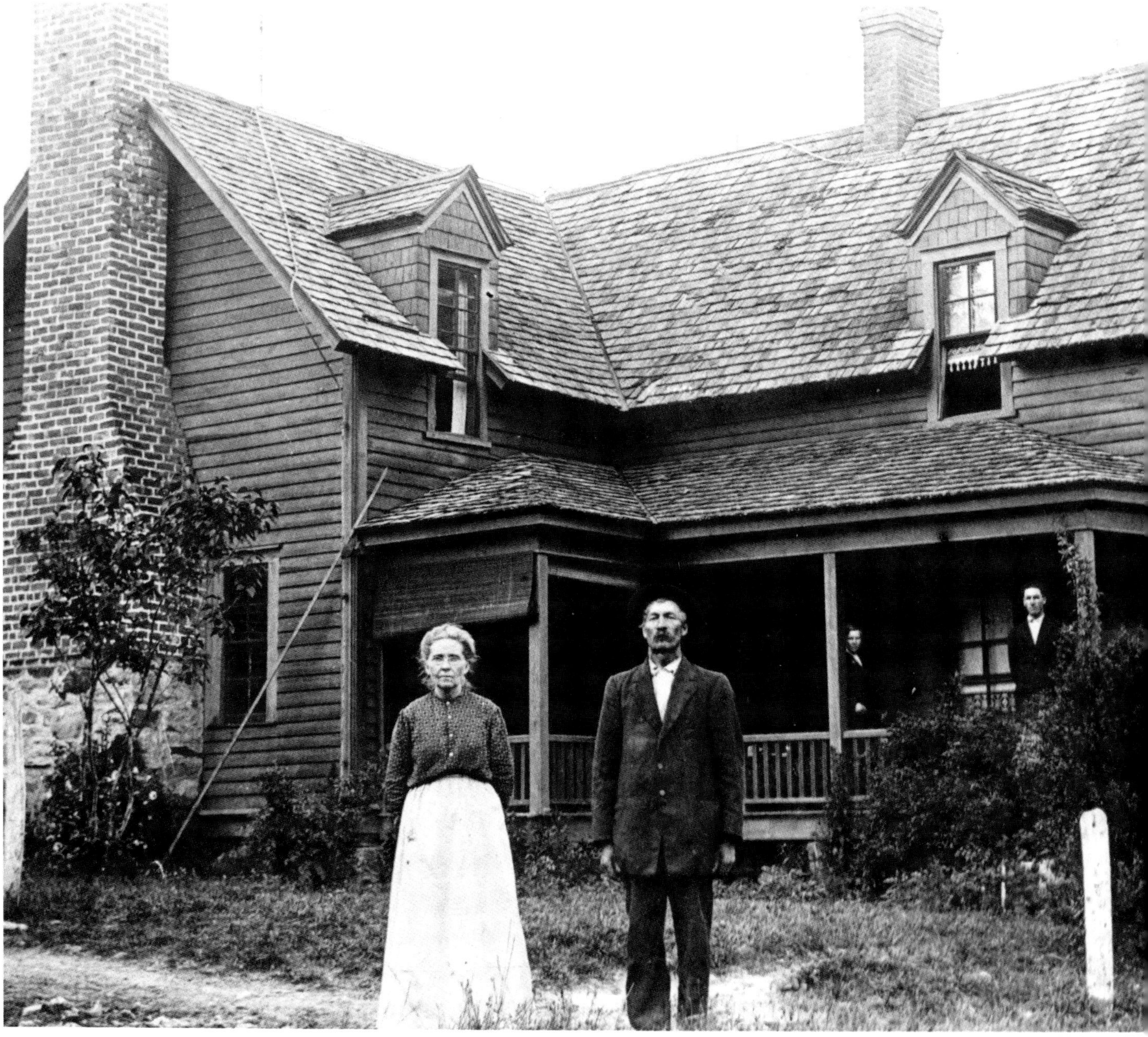

Buncombe Meets the World
1830 to 1850

When North Carolina opened Buncombe County for land grants, two types responded, the settler and the investor. Of the settlers, many families are living today on land issued to their ancestors by land grant. The investors, on the other hand, were speculators. In some cases they bought as much as a million acres of mountain land for twenty-five cents per acre and resold it.

Most people were self-sufficient farmers, even those who worked in town. They grew enough food for their families and raised livestock. James McConnell Smith, who owned land next to Public Square in 1830, grazed his cattle around the brick courthouse built in that year.

In their book, *From Ulster to Carolina*, Curtis Wood and Tyler Blethen said the Scotch-Irish practiced mixed farming. They grew wheat and corn, raised livestock, and hunted wild game. As the Indians had, they sold furs, feathers, beeswax, herbs, and roots.

A market for corn grew up around the drovers. On the old road up the French Broad, built as early as 1795, stock men called drovers herded large flocks of turkeys, cattle, or hogs through Buncombe County and Saluda Gap to markets in South Carolina and Georgia. To accommodate them, stands or inns opened along their route, places where men and animals were fed and housed each night.

Those who saw this animal drive remembered great numbers of animals crossing Public Square in Asheville, perhaps 150,000 hogs a season. These drives continued until the coming of railroads in Tennessee.

Those who invested in the Buncombe Turnpike, which opened in 1828, saw their wealth increase as travelers from South Carolina and elsewhere rode stagecoaches along the route. With the Buncombe Turnpike and the Western Turnpike coming together in Asheville in 1850, the county began to take its place as a regional center.

Facing page:
One of the oldest houses in the county still stands on Monte Vista Road, though it would be hard to recognize from this picture, made about 1910. The original story and a half with the large brick chimney was built about 1830 by John Thrash, Jr., and his wife Lucinda Yountz Thrash. Surrounding it was a large farm and orchard. Tradition is that one occupant, Augustus Buckingham Thrash, was so famous for his apple jack that a folk song was written about it.

> *"Cindy, where'd you get your whiskey?*
> *Where'd you get your dram?*
> *Got't from old man Elledge,*
> *Down at Buckingham's."*

The family says the porch and the addition to the right may have been added in the 1880s. Pictured are Hattie Thrash and her husband Richard Monroe Holcombe. On the porch are their sons Glenn and Theron Augustus. Richard ran Holcombe's Perennial Seed Company from the granary which is still on the property. Glenn and his wife Blanche Davis Holcombe removed the addition and added an inside kitchen. Photograph courtesy of Blanche Davis Holcombe.

James Gudger's son Samuel Bell Gudger and his wife Elizabeth Lowry Gudger moved from Turkey Creek to a hillside near Hominy Creek about 1832 to help Gudger's aunt Stacy Young Webb take care of her farm. In 1840 they built this house which still stands on Candler School Road, and brought up a family of eight children. According to Cabins and Castles, the extension to the left was added to the original house by the Gudger's daughter Eva Lane after she was married in 1877 to Jasper Young. Photograph courtesy of Charles M. Rice.

A painting of Tabernacle Meeting House, circa 1837, in Black Mountain was done by Martha Raines from a sketch by Mrs. Robert Davidson. According to a history of Black Mountain written in 1933 by the senior history class of Black Mountain High School, both Baptists and Methodists used this building for worship. It also may have housed the school mentioned in an old record dated November 25, 1848, signed by committeemen J. M. Hemphill, William Stepp, and Fletcher Fortune. The record states that "J. C. Jarvis taught the school for the space of three months of each year, for which he was paid a salary of sixteen dollars a month. The rudimentary subjects taught by Mr. Jarvis were reading, writing and arithmetic." Photograph courtesy of the Valley Museum, Black Mountain.

When the Ivy Township was being developed about 1800, Solomon Carter moved there with his parents. In 1816 he was married to Alvira Hopper and began to buy land, acquiring between three and four thousand acres. In 1823 he built the log core of this house pictured. Solomon Carter was firm in his political beliefs, so much so that he named the area where he lived Democrat. Photograph courtesy of Big Ivy Community Club.

Future governor Zebulon Vance was six years old in 1836 when he and his family boarded at the Nehemiah Blackstock home. The house was demolished in the 1980s when the Barnardsville exit was built off U.S. 23. Cordelia Camp in her book Governor Vance recalls a story from young Zeb's school master Matthew Woodson of Flat Creek. Woodson was trying to keep Zeb from cussing. After an outburst of profane language from Zeb, the schoolmaster gave the boy a pair of tongs, placed him beside a mouse hole in the corner of the school room, and ordered him not to open his mouth until he caught a mouse. Zeb sat by the hole while the work of the one-room school went on. When it came time for "spelling by heart," he had been forgotten. All at once he startled the school by shouting, "Dammed if I haven't got him!" In this later picture of the house, the appealing little girls in the foreground are not identified. Photograph courtesy of Dry Ridge Museum, Weaverville.

A Presbyterian assembly known as Robert Patton's Meeting House is said to be the first established church in Buncombe County. The meetinghouse for that first group of Bee Tree residents was about one-half mile east of this present building, built in 1839. The church is now known as Piney Grove Presbyterian Church. Photograph courtesy of Valley Museum, Black Mountain.

If Buncombe County residents could afford it, they sent their children to private schools, like Newton, Colonel Lee's, or Ravenscroft. Ravenscroft operated in this handsome brick house which Joseph Osborne built as a residence about 1840. He is thought to have been a successful storekeeper in business with James Patton. Ravenscroft School was established in 1855 by the Protestant Episcopal Church with the Reverend Jarvis Buxton as principal. At the close of the Civil War the school was reorganized and operated as a diocesan school for boys. A Mr. Schoenberger, a northerner, gave eleven thousand dollars for the erection of a building to be used as a training school for the ministry. Ravenscroft, located near downtown Asheville, is now used for a family health center. It is one of the oldest houses in Asheville. Photograph from the North Carolina Collection, Pack Memorial Public Library.

A classic cottage was built in the Beaverdam settlement by Wally Killian in 1840. This house still stands on Beaverdam Road near the Asbury United Methodist Church. Wally Killian was the son of Daniel Killian who came to Beaverdam before the census of 1790. Photograph courtesy of Historic Resources Commission.

One of the earliest graveyards in Downtown Asheville was south of the Presbyterian Church on Church Street. In it, according to Foster Sondley in the History of Buncombe County, were graves moved from an earlier burial ground located near Public Square at what is today Eagle and Market streets. Many of Asheville's leading citizens were buried in the Presbyterian graveyard from 1844 until Riverside Cemetery was opened in 1885. All the graves were moved to Riverside except that of early settler James Patton, which was under the Church Street library building. Patton, with Samuel Chunn, had deeded the land on which the graveyard and church were located. Photograph from the North Carolina Collection, Pack Memorial Public Library.

In the mid-nineteenth century, wealthy planters from the Charleston area began responding to the advertising of those who had bought speculation land in Western North Carolina. Most of the large tracts of land the South Carolinians purchased were in Henderson County; however, South Buncombe came in for its share of notice. One of the largest plantations belonged to Alexander Robinson, who purchased 1500 acres near the Henderson County line about 1850. Robinson built a pillared home, true to Southern tradition, which he named Struan. In 1900 a preparatory school for young men, Christ School, was founded on the Robinson plantation by the Reverend Thomas Wetmore of the Episcopal Church. Photograph from the Library of Congress, used courtesy of James H. Coman.

William Coleman succeeded his father-in-law George Swain as postmaster at Asheville from 1827 to 1842. About 1850, tired of life in town, he moved to Reems Creek to a place later called Warsaw and built a mill and a hat factory. The mill was at the site of the old Baird or Lane Iron Works. His mill ground corn and flower and extracted linseed oil from flax seed. Bascom Lotspeich, who later owned the mill site, named the lake "Louise" for his wife. Photograph courtesy of Dry Ridge Museum, Weaverville.

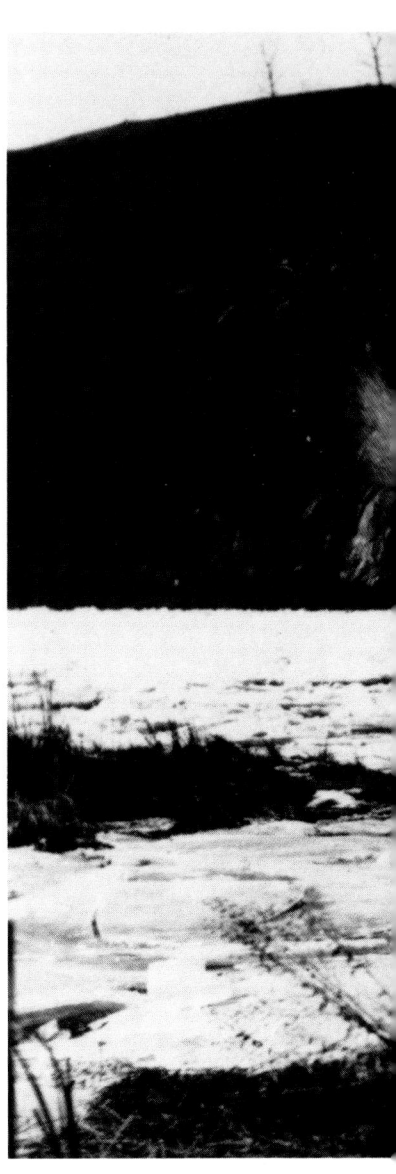

Dr. Frederick Blake bought the house in South Buncombe, now Royal Pines, which Joseph B. Pyatt had built in 1847. Blake named it Newington. He was the son of Daniel Blake, a wealthy South Carolina rice planter who owned vast acres of land in South Buncombe, part of which became Henderson County in 1838. Called the Blake House today, this building serves as a bed and breakfast hostelry. Picture courtesy of James H. Coman.

Before the days of manufactured ice, those who could afford to do so dug pits on their property and gathered ice when the rivers and farm ponds froze. These icehouses were often fifteen feet deep and men would get into them with ladders. Straw was used for insulation. Dr. Sondley makes great claims for the severity of the winters in the early days. He said that in the second quarter of the nineteenth century ice on the French Broad River supported a four-horse wagon with a load of hay. In this picture the river seems to be frozen so solid that ice floes have been pushed onto the bank. Photograph courtesy of the North Carolina Collection, Pack Memorial Public Library.

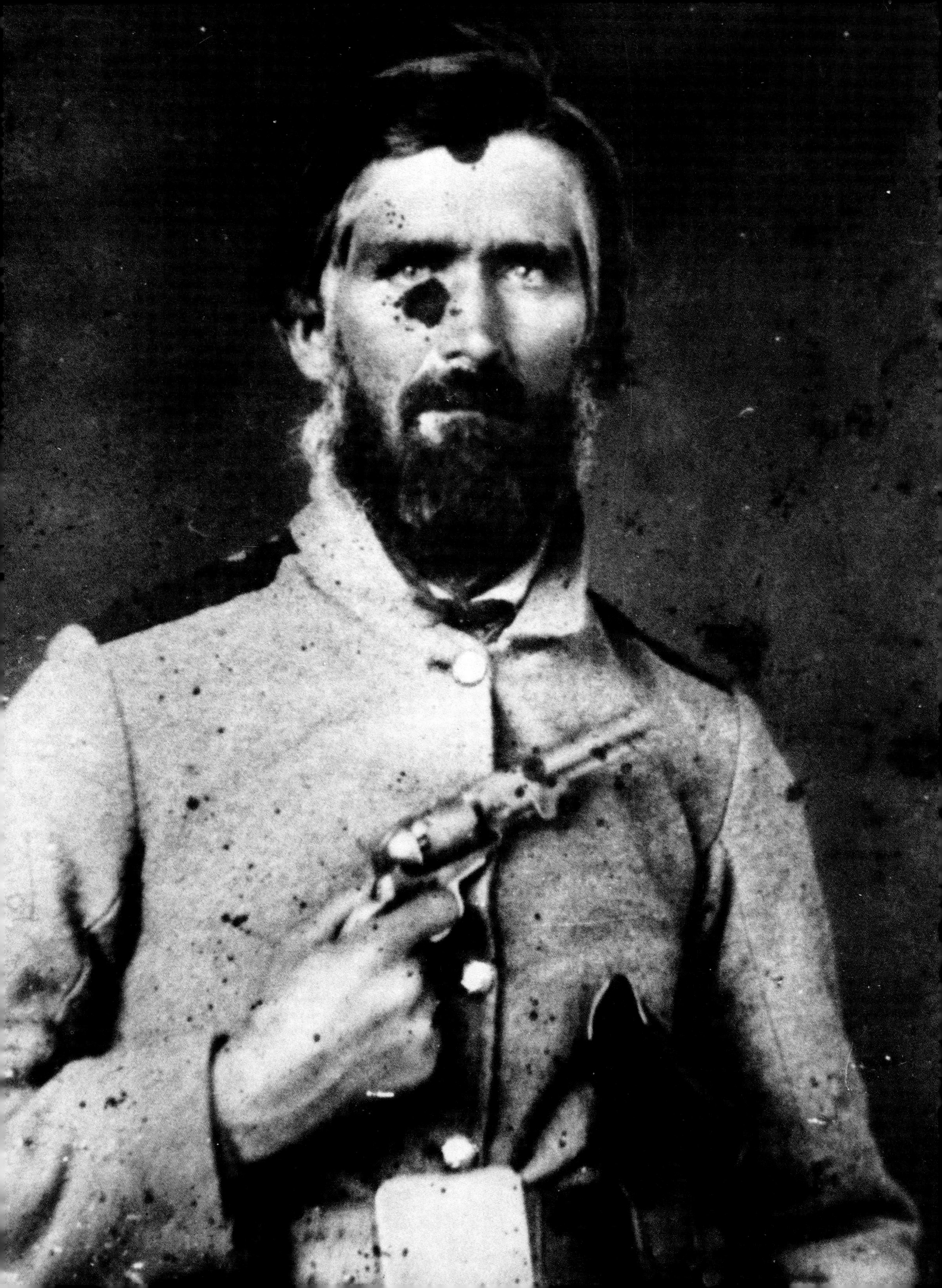

A County Divided

1850 to 1875

An influx of new people and ideas into the county changed its nature. Fine homes began to appear in Asheville and along its fringes. The county's second brick courthouse was built in 1850. That year the population of Buncombe was 13,425. There was even talk of a railroad.

The coming of the Civil War was a disaster. Money and energies were diverted. On Public Square the Confederacy opened a hospital, a commissary, and a post office. Asheville was being touted as the "Capital of the Confederacy," as men from the western counties marched through Swannanoa Gap to catch the train at Salisbury. But in the county many had no sentiments for seccession. Feelings ran high as brother marched against brother.

One small skirmish north of Asheville pulled old men and young boys of the home guard into the fray. The worse damage in remote areas was done by renegades from both sides who hid in the mountains and raided isolated farms.

Manpower was in short supply, crops were confiscated to feed soldiers, and wild game was no longer plentiful. Poverty among the mountain people was rampant. The only hope lay with the "bright yellow" tobacco market that opened in 1870 and lasted until 1897. During that time Asheville had its own warehouses and farmers raised as much as seven million pounds of tobacco in one year.

Men from the North Carolina Militia in Buncombe County were called to assist with the removal of the Cherokee Indians in the western counties in 1838. Capt. Wesley Duckett of the Sandy Mush community, age 21, served in this capacity. When he was 45, Duckett marched with the Confederate Army but returned home the next year because of a fever. Duckett was never able to return to action. Photograph courtesy of Mabel Duckett.

At the time of the Civil War many mountain people had no cause for which to fight. Slaves were not part of their life, the interests of the state affected them little. They were content to stay on the farm and work toward survival for themselves and their families. Therefore, it was not uncommon for them avoid to conscription by the Army of the Confederacy if possible, even to the point of going over the Tennessee line and joining the Union forces. This split the loyalties sometimes separated family members or caused feuds among neighbors. James Asberry Duckett, from Worley Cove in Sandy Mush, was the son of Wesley Duckett. James was drafted by Confederate forces, also, but deserted twice. Finally, he joined the Union Army. Duckett returned to Sandy Mush after the war and became a shoemaker. He is shown with Nora Burress Duckett, his second wife. Photograph courtesy of Mabel Duckett.

Wesley and Margaret "Peggy" Crawford Duckett raised a big family, most of whom remained in the Sandy Mush community. In this family portrait made about 1870 are, front row, left to right, Margaret, Hariett Louisa, Saray An, Merenda Jane, and Maudie. Back row, left to right, Arlious, James Asberry, Wesley, Edward, and Phyletus. Photograph courtesy of Mabel Duckett.

With eight sons in the Civil War, the Stevens family may have set a record. This portrait was made in 1894 of the Stevens and their sister Nancy Stevens Penland. Seated left to right are Dr. J. Mitchell Stevens, Thomas N., Nancy, and David M. Standing are Merritt, Francis, Jesse, Robert, and Alfred. Alfred was 16 when he joined in 1864. Mitchell, a surgeon, was 30. In the harshness of the war two of the brothers were wounded and one taken prisoner. The Stevens returned to Asheville and led successful careers. Photograph courtesy of Jack Stevens.

Levi Plemmons made medical history in Buncombe County. After serving in the Army of the Confederacy in the Civil War, Plemmons returned to marry Martha Hayes of the Newfound community and settle down in Turkey Creek. His was the life of a farmer, but he did serve a term as sheriff of Buncombe County. Then, Plemmons developed cancer. The doctor removed his eye, but that didn't stop the disease. Plemmons made medical history when he went north to a hospital and allowed doctors there to remove the side of his face and replace it with silver. Photograph courtesy of Levi Hall.

45

Brigadier General James G. Martin was in command of the Western North Carolina forces during the last days of the Civil War and was party to one of the last surrenders. According to Ora Blackmun's history, a cavalry unit under Brig. Gen. Alvan C. Gillim rode through Hickory Nut Gorge accompanied by Gen. George W. Kirk's volunteers on April 25, 1865, more than two weeks after Gen. Robert E. Lee had surrendered at Appomatox. General Martin met the forces at Busbee and in his surrender agreed to furnish the troops with a three-day ration if they would leave the county in peace. The cavalry accepted his terms, but the next morning a small unit returned to wreak havoc in Asheville. Several buildings were destroyed: the gun factory, General Martin's house, and the home of Robert H. Chapman, minister of the Presbyterian Church. Federal forces roamed the countryside, taking animals and food from the farms. The Martins became active citizens of Asheville following the war. He and Col. T. W. Patton were leading promoters of the Asheville Street Railway Company, chartered by the state in 1881. Photograph courtesy of the North Carolina Department of Archives and History.

The aftermath of the Civil War forced on the citizens of Buncombe changes that disturbed their way of life. One was giving the blacks the right to vote. Whether it's a cartoon or an actual drawing of events as seen through the eyes of an artist, this picture ran in an 1867 Harper's Magazine labeled Asheville, N.C. It is supposedly a scene of blacks lined up on Public Square to register. The jubilation of the young dancing man brings to mind a story told by an Ashevillian. When word arrived about the Emancipation Proclamation, he stood on the upper porch of the Carolina House and watched blacks parading up North Main Street singing "Glory, glory, we is free, we is free." Every account describes reconstruction as a difficult time for both races. Photograph courtesy of North Carolina Collection, Pack Memorial Public Library.

Contractor E. J. Armstrong came to Asheville from Connecticut in the late 1870s to recover from tuberculosis and purchased this home in Chunn's Cove on the grounds of Col. Stephen Lee's private school. Before his retirement Armstrong bought much property in Asheville on which he built homes. The house in this photograph was taken down in 1917. Photograph courtesy of Eugenia Ray Carter.

This house and the one purchased by the Armstrongs in the 1870s were on the campus of the school operated by Col. Stephen Lee. Lee, a West Point graduate, came to Asheville in 1849 and opened a school near the Swannanoa River, about where the Cloister Condominiums are now. Later, he moved the school to these buildings in Chunn's Cove. Except for a short interruption during the Civil War, the school continued until Colonel Lee's death in 1869. This house, which served as a dormitory, stood until the 1920s. Photograph courtesy of Eugenia Ray Carter.

When the Reverend Alfred M. Penland returned to his home on Reems Creek in 1870 after several years of work with the Presbyterian Church in the north, he brought with him the Presbyterian zeal to preach and to teach mountain people. The log house shown here is where the Reverend Mr. Penland was born in 1833. With him are members of his family. The young man in the foreground is his son F. A. Penland, who gained respect as an educator in county schools. For many years children from the Beech community attended primary school in this house. Photograph courtesy of "Pat" Rhea Hensley.

Asheville's public library began in 1870 when a group of women gathered books together and placed them in a reading room on South Main Street, now Biltmore Avenue. When the courthouse was constructed in 1876, the reading room opened on the third floor there. The library moved to its own building next to the Presbyterian Church on Church Street in 1893, but it came back to the Square when George Pack bought the First National Bank Building on the southeast corner in 1899 and donated it to the Asheville Library Board. Photograph from the North Carolina Collection, Pack Memorial Public Library.

An early photograph of South Main Street (now Biltmore Avenue) shot looking south from Public Square, clears up the question of where the Bank Hotel was located, as indicated in Asheville, a Pictorial History. On the southwest corner of Public Square was a building known as Hilliard Hall, built and operated as a hotel by James Mitchell Alexander. At some point, it was also called the Bank Hotel, because the Asheville Branch of the Bank of Cape Fear, the community's first bank, adjoined it on the east. Dr. P. C. Lester, a physician, operated a drug store here after 1850. Photograph from the North Carolina Collection, Pack Memorial Public Library.

Arden House was the family home of Charles Willing Beale and family. Beale came to the Limestone area in the 1870s, built Arden House, and named it for the Forest of Arden in Shakespeare's As You Like It. Near his home he built Arden Park Hotel which served as a stagecoach inn until the arrival of the railroad. He also laid out the community of Arden. Beale was a writer of mystery novels and philosophical articles. Mrs. Beale was a founder of the Edward Buncombe Chapter of the American Daughters of the Revolution. She enjoyed painting. The Beales filled their home with a collection of fine art. Photograph courtesy of Bertha Fletcher Holland.

Weaverville College, located at the corner of Lake Shore Drive and College Street in Weaverville, was chartered in 1873. In 1883 the property was deeded to the Methodist Episcopal Church South. The first building, the Administration Building, was ready for students in 1874. An addition in 1895 almost doubled its capacity. A boarding school, the Masonic and Temperance High School, first stood on property later used by Weaverville College. When that academy burned in 1872, the community felt strongly that it should be replaced with another educational institution. As an economic move in 1934 the Methodist church combined Weaverville College with Brevard College. In its sixty-one-year history Weaverville had served students from first grade through college. Many children whose home communities had no high school owe their education to Weaverville College. Photograph courtesy of Dry Ridge Museum, Weaverville.

Reems Creek Presbyterian Church celebrated its bicentennial in 1991, claiming to be one of the oldest churches in the county, with George Newton, early preacher and school teacher, as its first minister. Richard Morris Hunt, who designed the Biltmore House, is said to be the architect of the present building and manse shown here in the early 1930s. Photograph courtesy of "Pat" Rhea Hensley.

Dr. James Americus Reagan came to Buncombe County on horseback in 1850 with other Methodist preachers to take churches on the Asheville Circuit. He married Mary Weaver of Reems Creek and spent the rest of his life as a minister and medical doctor in the North Buncombe area. Dr. Reagan is said to have delivered 986 children in his career as a physician and a surgeon. In addition to church and medical offices, he was a founder and first president of Weaverville College, eight years on the Buncombe County Board of Commissioners, secretary of Board of Education, and mayor of Weaverville. Photograph courtesy of Dry Ridge Museum, Weaverville.

Brush Hill School on the Old Farm School Road was one of six rural schools maintained by the Peabody Educational Fund in 1874. Prior to the district tax levies for schools in 1887, a measure that passed by only two votes, the Peabody Fund contributed eighteen hundred dollars a year to each school that would stay open ten months. Brush Hill was built on land donated by Joseph H. Rice. Rice's well served the schoolhouse. Photograph courtesy of Frances Shaffer.

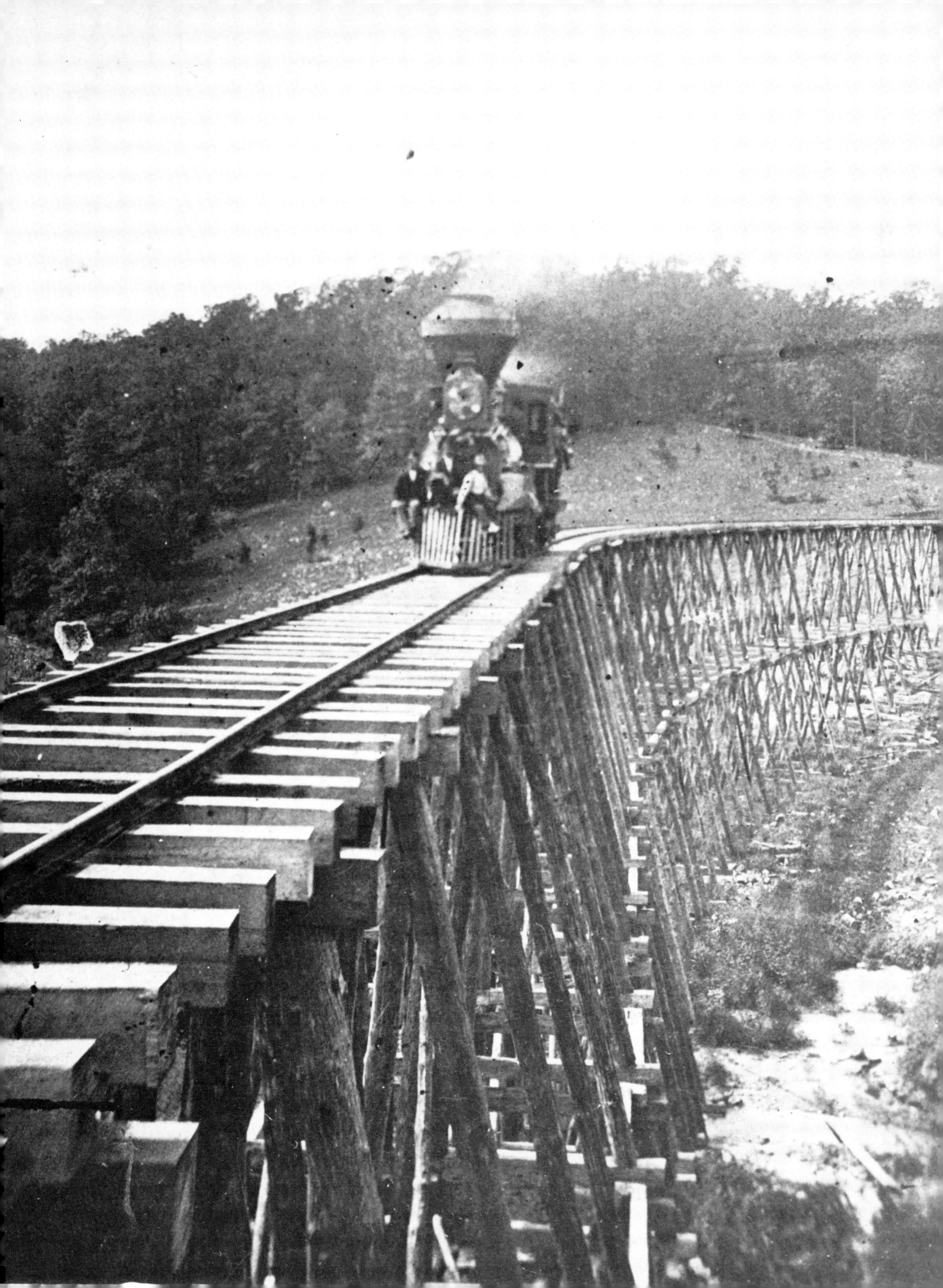

Growth Rode the Rails

5

1875 to 1890

Hope for Buncombe rode on the first train to conquer the Blue Ridge Mountains in the spring of 1879. With railroads branching in four directions, what had been an isolated mountain county became, by 1891, a rail hub for the south.

Tourists and sick people rode "the cars." Sanitariums for tubercular patients dotted the hillsides. Specialists who came for their own cure stayed to widen the county's reputation as a health center.

Fancy hotels and boarding houses that catered to fancy people demanded fruits and vegetables and dairy products from local farmers. Truck farming and fruit production increased as the county population and the number of part-time residents grew. A cigar factory, a woolen mill, and a cotton mill used farm products and provided non-farm jobs.

The county built a brick courthouse with a opera house in the upper story in 1876. In the summer there was entertainment every night. Public Square was a busy place. Every lawyer who made the circuit of county seats with the Superior Court of North Carolina had an office in Asheville.

Still, everyday life on the farm changed little. The public school system had been a victim of war. Running water, electricity, telephones, street cars, and paved roads were marvels to be seen in town by the 1890s, but in the country, oxen still pulled the homemade plows.

In October 1880 the trestle over Gashes Creek was completed and the first small engine steamed into Asheville. The diamond stacked wood-burner shown here may be the Little Salisbury, *the engine that was pulled by oxen and mules over a mountain so the Swannanoa tunnel could be worked from both sides. The cutting and drying of timbers and the building of this trestle was a Herculean task. Also, because this engine ran on wood, it belched forth sparks and fire as it went and is said to have caught the woods on fire along the way. Gashes Creek is located near the River Ridge Factory Outlet in East Asheville. Photograph courtesy of Historic Resources Commission.*

Point Tunnel on the Western North Carolina Railroad crossed Mill Creek on the eastern slope of the Blue Ridge, the first of seven tunnels needed to conquer the mountain. John Ager in Cabins and Castles said that at the height of the construction 1,455 men, 403 boys, and over 1,000 mules, horses, and oxen were employed. Tunnels were dug by hand. For blasting the men used a new substance called nitroglycerine and mixed it with sawdust or cornmeal. Wagons or small engines carried debris. Bridges were built of cut stones and concrete. When the Swannanoa, the longest and last tunnel, broke through on March 11, 1879, Maj. James W. Wilson, construction engineer wired Gov. Zebulon Vance, "Daylight entered Buncombe County today through Swannanoa Tunnel. Grade and centers met exactly." Photograph courtesy of James H. Coman.

Building the Western North Carolina Railroad from Henry's Station to Asheville was perilous for the men involved, many of them convicts from prisons further east. Mud Cut between Old Fort and Ridgecrest continued to slide until about 1900 when the cut was widened around the "white mud" and another track installed. This siding was named for Col. Thad Coleman of Buncombe County, construction engineer on Mud Cut. In his novel The Road, author John Ehle, who grew up in Asheville, describes a scene in which the white mud buried an engine with the engineer aboard. The next day three hundred men with mules and oxen manned chains and poles and pulled the engine out. Photograph from the North Carolina Collection, Pack Memorial Public Library.

Dating a picture is like solving a puzzle. Dr. Sondley's history said a few gas lamps lighted Public Square before the first electricity in 1888. He also describes paving of the "city center" with rock taken from the site of the reservoir about 1884. Photograph from the North Carolina Collection, Pack Memorial Public Library.

Since about 1875 Fernihurst has stood on a hilltop overlooking the French Broad River and the mountains beyond. Writers from the nineteenth century spoke eloquently as they described the view from Connally's hill. It's even been said that George Vanderbilt tried to buy Fernihurst before he developed the Biltmore property. The Reverend John Kerr Connally, who built Fernihurst, gave up his law practice after a religious experience, became a minister, and moved to Buncombe County from Richmond, Virginia. The house was built for a summer house, but the family spent several months a year there and became active members of Asheville's society. Fernihurst, now located on the property of Asheville Buncombe Technical Community College, was named for the Kerr family castle in Scotland. Photograph from the North Carolina Collection, Pack Memorial Public Library.

A traveler of the early 1800s was photographed as he sat on the bank of the river enjoying his lunch. The valise on which he sat indicates that he is, perhaps, a traveling salesman, a "drummer" as they were called. His photograph, as many other colorful ones, became a stereoscopic image to be sold. It may have turned up in a family's parlor to be viewed through their prized stereoscope. Photograph from the North Carolina Collection, Pack Memorial Public Library.

Facing page bottom:
The Turnpike Hotel stood for over 150 years on what was originally called the Western Turnpike. A book published in 1883, From the Heart of the Alleghanies of Western North Carolina, describes the hotel. "Sixteen miles east of Asheville in a model country hotel, at Turnpike. For long years it was a noonday stopping place for the stages on the way from Asheville to Wanesville (sic). Since the railroad began operation it has become a station, and when we first came through from the West it was the breakfast place for the passengers. It is situated at the head of Hominy valley, amid pleasant mountain surrounds. John C. Smathers, the genial, rotund proprietor, will, with his pleasant wife and daughters, render the tourist's stay so agreeable that the intended week of sojourn here may be lengthened into a month. John C. is a representative country man. What place he actually fills in the small settlement at Turnpike, can be best illustrated by giving the reported cross-examination which he underwent one day at the hands of an inquisitive traveler:
"Mr. Smathers," said this traveler, "are you the proprietor of this hotel?"
"Yes, sir."
"Who is the postmaster here?"
"I am."
"Who keeps the store?"
"I do."
"Who runs the blacksmith shop?"
"I do."
"How about the mill?"
"Ditto."
"Anything else?"
"Well, I have something of a farm, let me tell you."
"And as a Christian?"
"I am a pillar in the Methodist church; the father of thirteen children; and my sons and sons-in-law just about run the neighboring county-seat." As the book said, Smathers was typical of the many innkeepers who carried over from stagecoach days. Photograph courtesy of Eleanor N. Rice.

A dream of making the French Broad River like the mighty Mississippi and Asheville the New Orleans of the East ran aground with the Mountain Lily in the 1880s. The ninety-foot, two-paddle sidewheeler with two decks was the dream of a group of men from Henderson, Transylvania, and Buncombe counties who formed a stock company and sold shares for twenty-five dollars each. When the boat was completed, it made a few trips to Brevard. It stayed on the river for excursions until it ran aground. There is no record of its reaching Asheville. Photograph from the North Carolina Collection, Pack Memorial Public Library.

Asheville became a hub for the railroads after 1886, and stagecoaches no longer ran over familiar routes. Soon fine hotels were catering to the railroad traffic, among them the Mountain Park Hotel in Warm Springs, now called Hot Springs. In 1886 the Southern Improvement Company bought the springs and built the hotel. The springs in Hot Springs are still active and a new hotel is planned. Photograph from the North Carolina Collection, Pack Memorial Public Library.

This etching found in an old book, From the Heart of the Alleghanies of Western North Carolina by Zeigler and Grosseup, published in 1883, is entitled "Mount Pisgah with West Asheville in the foreground." No identification is given beyond that. If the river in the foreground is the French Broad, the bridge may be Smith's bridge, the first known bridge across the river. Photograph from the North Carolina Collection, Pack Memorial Public Library.

Pleasant Grove Church on Pleasant Grove Road near Weaverville is unique because it is one of the few union Protestant churches in the county. Land for the original church was granted in 1880 by James M. and Matilda Parker and R. G. and Lucinda Brank. This first building, built of slabs and logs, was used as both church and school, known as Slab College. Presbyterians, Methodists, and Baptists held services. A new building was begun in 1940 when one of the members and her grandson carried two rocks and placed them at the church. A friend donated $5. Thus, according to the congregation, "with two rocks, $5, and a lot of faith" a new building was built. Photograph courtesy of "Pat" Rhea Hensley.

Probably influenced by Dr. J. W. Gleitsmann's reports of the salubrious effects of a mountain climate on tuberculosis, Dr. Karl Von Ruck came to Asheville in 1886 to study the tubercle bacillus. In 1886 he opened Winyah Sanitarium on East Street, but he turned it over to his son Silvio to administer and gave his attentions to the development of an effective anti-tuberculosis vaccine. In 1918 Silvio went to New England to administer the vaccine to children in an orphanage and died of influenza in New York City. On the way home Silvio's daughter died of the same disease. Dr. Karl Von Ruck retired to his mansion and died a year later. He had helped establish Asheville as a health center, however, because of the number of specialists who came to study with him and stayed to practice in the city. Photograph from the North Carolina Collection, Pack Memorial Public Library.

In 1882 Asheville city fathers gave official sanction to a volunteer fire department, but it was over ten years before the department acquired its first hook and ladder truck. The city's eleven firemen and a driver are posed in front of the City Hall, built at the east end of Public Square in 1892. Photograph courtesy of the North Carolina Collection, Pack Memorial Public Library.

A large crew turned out for a workday at Bethel Methodist Episcopal Church South on Riceville Road. This building, erected in 1888, burned in 1923. The third building, the present Bethel Church, was dedicated in 1970. Most of this work crew has been identified. They are, top step, Will Glass; next step, left to right, Harlie Allison, Callie Allison Champion, William Riley Ray, and Nellie Allison Hughey Deweese; on the ground, unidentified woman with child and little boy, Dilla Ray Penley, Lela Allison Meredith, William Newton "Kirk" Creasman, Millard Head, Jim Meredith, Jesse Alexander Ray, Lloyd Glass, and Jack Meredith. Photograph courtesy of Eugenia Ray Carter.

Leonard P. Miller said in his history of the schools that there is evidence a school existed in the Sand Hill community as early as 1789. It is known, however, that in 1840 Charles Moore, son of Capt. William Moore, erected a frame school building there and the Reverend Jacob Hood taught Sand Hill Academy. The two-room brick building pictured was on land deeded to the local school committee by Dr. and Mrs. D. M. Gudger in 1884 for what is thought to be the first public school in Buncombe County. Photograph courtesy of William Henry.

This family grouping on College Street circa 1889 can bring to mind all kind of images. The Ray family lived on Grassy Branch in the Riceville section. Imagine the long wagon ride to town with that many little boys, keeping them "slicked up" for their picture. Shown left to right are Jesse Alexander and Sophronia Creasman Ray with twins Martin and Marvin, Charlotte Ida, Lona Belle, Charles Sherman, James Albert, John, and William Festus. The family has no explanation for the tent in the background. Picture courtesy of Eugenia Ray Carter.

Since waters with minerals in them were thought to have curative powers, pioneer school teacher Robert Henry must have seen his discovery of the sulphur springs west of Asheville as a goldmine. According to history, he discovered it in 1827 when he and his body servant Sam were making a trip through the county. Henry and his son-in-law Col. Reuben Deaver built a large frame hotel at the springs about 1830 which was highly patronized by visitors from the low country. The Deaver Hotel burned in 1862. In 1887 E. G. Carrier built the brick hotel shown here at the site and operated a streetcar to it. The car crossed the French Broad River on Carrier Bridge, which was located near the conflux of the Swannanoa and French Broad rivers. In 1891 this building also was destroyed by fire. These hotels were located in the vicinity of Asheville School for Boys. Photograph courtesy of the North Carolina Collection, Pack Memorial Public Library.

On a hilltop high above Biltmore Avenue, on land donated to the Presbyterian Church U.S.A. by the Reverend and Mrs. Louis M. Pease, the Home Industrial School for Girls opened in 1887. The Reverend Pease wrote in the Home Mission Monthly of 1889 that "the way to turn poor mountain white children into hard-working Christian patriots would be to take them from their home influences and home-formed habits and subject them to a steady, strong, and prudent discipline." The school became a noted college for educating teachers, the Normal and Collegiate Institute. In 1940 the Normal School closed. Florence Stephenson Hall, named for the school's first principal, became Asheville Biltmore College, Victoria Hospital, and then, Memorial Mission Hospital. It was razed in 1982 when additions were made to Mission. Photograph courtesy of James H. Coman.

With dinner "on the ground," members of Montmorencie (sic) Methodist Episcopal Church South celebrated in 1888 the dedication of this building on Pisgah Highway. A 1957 booklet says this, their second church building, stood on three and one/half acres of land bought from B. L. Morgan for $69.82. Trustee J. W. Rice made the bricks on his land and hauled them to the church site in wagons. Wooden boxes served as molds, four bricks to a mold. The boxes were filled with mud, sprinkled with sand, and burned in a kiln. Montmorenci United Methodist Church was updated with the addition of an educational wing in 1949 and a sanctuary in 1963. Photograph by James W. Rice, used courtesy of Charles M. Rice.

After John Evans Brown acquired property on Beaucatcher Mountain in 1840, he went to New Zealand to find his fortune as a sheep rancher. In 1889 he returned to the county and built a stone castle on a site that commanded an outstanding view of the Swannanoa Valley. He named his home Zealandia. When Brown died, Philip S. Henry, an internationally known diplomat, scholar, and art collector moved into Zealandia. Henry built a Tudor house beside the castle and opened an art gallery there, from 1924 to 1930. The stone castle was taken down in the 1950s but the Tudor house remains. It is now the corporate headquarters of Peppertree Resorts, Limited. Photograph courtesy of the North Carolina Collection, Pack Memorial Public Library.

Picturesque Payne's Chapel stands on a bluff at the foot of Earley's Mountain in Sandy Mush. Its parishoners are gone as of 1951, but an American flag waves in its graveyard in memory of a soldier killed in Vietnam. In 1889 Payne's Chapel was built on land donated by Malinda Payne to the Methodist Episcopal Church North. Picture by David Holt.

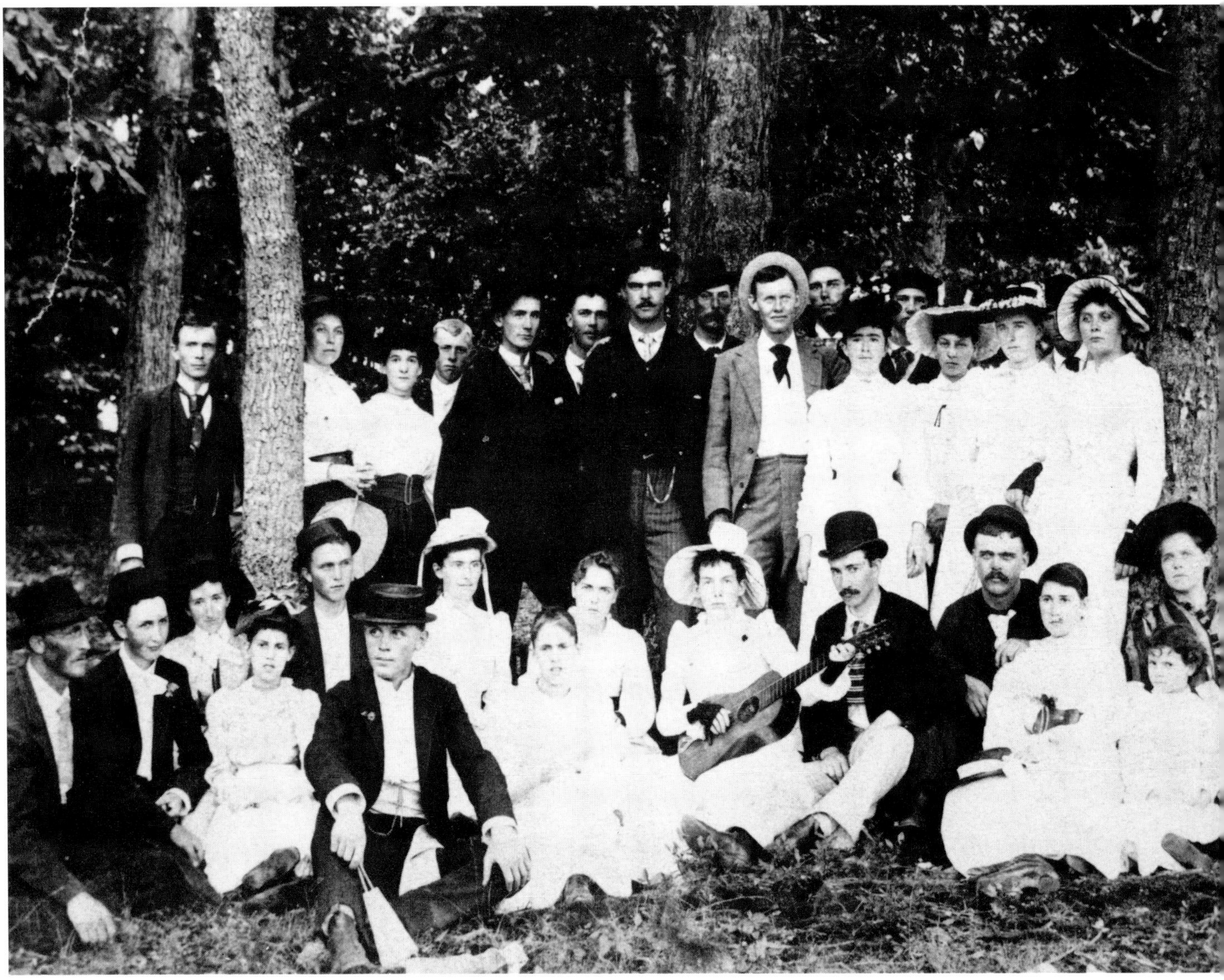

Incorporation Fever

1890 to 1900

6

Buncombe County turned one hundred in 1892, amid the birth of colleges, religion, and incorporation. George Vanderbilt awed the people with his mansion on the hills south of town.

Churches and other philanthropic organizations helped schools. District school taxes encouraged city and county school boards. Two years of teacher certification courses were offered in Weaverville, Black Mountain, Fairview, Leicester, Montreat, Swannanoa, and Asheville. Because some of these schools were religious institutions, they filled their summers with retreat programs. Montreat, Ridgecrest, Christmont, and other religious retreats outside Buncombe date back to the turn of the century.

Incorporation fever hit small communities. Some of them and their dates of incorporation are Leicester, 1874; Weaversville, 1875 (the "s" was dropped two years later); Black Mountain and Biltmore, 1893; South Biltmore, Arden, and Jupiter, 1895; Hazel and Buena Vista, 1891; Inanda, 1893, and Alexander, 1905. Except for Weaverville and Black Mountain these incorporations have been repealed.

To celebrate spring and the end of the 1892 school year these students from Mills River Academy went on a picnic. Notice the ladies' handmade bonnets. The second picture of some of the same people was made three years later. Fashion then dictated that the ladies wear store-bought hats. Photographs from the album of Ella Case, used courtesy of Marion Case Havener.

Frances Goodrich, a home missionary of the North Presbyterian Church, came to Buncombe County in 1890 and stayed for the rest of her life, giving herself to the betterment of life for mountain people. Goodrich came as a teacher, but her focus was widened when Mrs. William Davis of Brittains Cove near Weaverville showed her a handwoven lindsey-woolsey coverlet made of natural threads dyed with chestnut-oak bark. According to Dr. Jan Davidson in his introduction to Goodrich's book Mountain Homespun, the coverlet excited Goodrich and she began to develop a crafts industry. A commercial outlet, Allenstand, opened in Asheville in 1908. Goodrich was joined by other craftspersons and in 1929 the Southern Highland Handicraft Guild was formed. After years of work in the mountains Goodrich and her sister Julia moved to Asheville and continued working with causes which made life better for people. Photograph courtesy of Southern Highland Handicraft Guild.

George Willis Pack, the man whose name is known to every Buncombe County child because of Pack Square and Pack Library lived in the city only twenty years, from 1883 to 1903. His caring and generosity, however, have gone unrivaled. Mr. and Mrs. Pack moved to Asheville from Cleveland because she was suffering from a throat ailment. Within a short time Pack began using his wealth to support major projects, Vance Monument, the library, parks, and schools. Finally, before the Packs moved to Long Island to be nearer their son, they gave land for a new county courthouse. On January 8, 1901, the commissioners voted to accept his offer to "give to the county, to be used for a site for a court house and county offices, the land on College Street in Asheville, which I purchased from Col. A. T. Davidson, provided that the county will dedicate to the public, forever, to be used for the purposes of a public square, park, or place, whatever land the county may own within the limits of public square, so called, in Asheville, the present court house to be removed therefrom." A fifty-thousand-dollar bond issue passed in 1902 to build that courthouse. County offices remained there until the present building was completed in 1928. When County Commissioners removed the 1903 courthouse, the land became a public park. This portrait of Pack was photographed by L. L. Roush of New York and used by Tiffany to design a gold medal for the celebration of the Pack's golden wedding anniversary, June 24, 1904. When Pack died in 1906, he was buried in Cleveland, but a memorial service was held for him in the courthouse and the fire alarm bell on Pack Square tolled solemnly from three to four o'clock, the time of his funeral in Cleveland. Photograph from the North Carolina Collection, Pack Memorial Public Library.

Diplomat Richmond Pearson turned developer in 1890 when he completed the building of Richmond Hill, his Victorian mansion on the west side of the French Broad River. In order to prove that roads would open up his property, he brought about five thousand Buncombe County citizens to his hillside for a July Fourth celebration and paid a thousand men a dollar each to work on what would become Lakeshore Avenue. Pearson hired Asheville street railway system to transport people from Public Square to a train which brought them across the river. The train stopped at a site below "Lake Marjorie." For refreshments the crowd enjoyed lemonade or iced tea. After dark there were fireworks. Photograph from the North Carolina collection, Pack Memorial Public Library.

John Meyers Stepp grew up in the Swannanoa Valley, the son of a slave on the Joseph Stepp farm. Though without formal schooling, he became one of the most respected men in the valley. He lived to be 105 (1850-1955), raised a family, and sent all of his children to college. For thirty years he served on the school committee for Swannanoa schools. Photograph courtesy of the Valley Museum, Black Mountain.

The occasion must have been special for the ladies of the Charles Winfield Johnston family to wear their lovely lace dresses. When George Vanderbilt bought the Johnston property in Bent Creek about 1890, they moved to this frame house on Glenn Bridge Road in the Avery's Creek community. The Johnstons are, left to right: Walter, Edith, father Charles W., Meta, mother Avaline Lance, Margaret, and Samuel. Photo courtesy of Frenche Reid Kimzey.

Militia grounds, where a contingent of local men formed small military units and trained weekly, were required by North Carolina law when Buncombe County was formed in 1792. Many men boasted military titles because of their positions in the militia. Militia grounds remained an important place in every larger community until after the Civil War. Then, they became reunion grounds. This reunion of Confederate veterans was held at the militia grounds off Pisgah Highway in Hominy in the 1890s. Photograph courtesy of Maybre Candler Brenton.

A well-known figure in political and historic circles, Theodore Davidson presided at ceremonies held for the Centennial of Buncombe County, August 10, 1892. In the Civil War, Davidson left with the first unit called out in Asheville, the Buncombe Riflemen commanded by Maj. William Wallace McDowell, and served as an officer on the staff of Brig. Gen. Robert Vance. He returned to serve as a member of the North Carolina legislature for four terms, from 1885 to 1893, as state attorney general, mayor of Asheville, and presiding judge of Buncombe County Criminal Court. Davidson died June 11, 1931. Photograph courtesy of Virginia Ryman Morrison.

While he was building the Biltmore Estate, George Vanderbilt began to plan with his chief architect Richard Morris Hunt and resident architect Richard Sharp Smith for a manorial village to house artisans and servants. Vanderbilt purchased the village of Asheville Junction, or Best, so named for a railroad official, and commissioned Hunt to design the church. Hunt died in 1895, so Sharp continued the designs with the half-timber, pebbledash houses. A hospital, school, church, and a cottage craft industry added to the life of those who lived there. On the hill across the river loomed the first Kenilworth Inn, completed in 1890. This building burned in 1909. Photograph courtesy of the North Carolina Room, Pack Memorial Public Library.

When the Western North Carolina Railroad reached Black Mountain in 1879, industry and tourism boomed and lumbermen came to town to buy up the forests. One of the pioneer families of the Bee Tree settlement, the Burnetts opened a large sawmill and shipped out hundreds of board feet of hardwoods and pine to supply the needs of a growing nation. Photograph from the Valley Museum, Black Mountain.

Once a route for the Buncombe Turnpike, today's Victoria Road runs from Biltmore Avenue to the Swannanoa River. In the 1890s when this photograph was made, the "Town of Victoria" had become so fashionable that George Vanderbilt built several rent houses there. Photograph by Ray, courtesy of the Smith McDowell House.

This may have been one of the last pictures made of Sen. Zebulon Baird Vance before he died. Senator and Mrs. Vance entertained the surviving members of his Civil War unit, the Rough and Ready Guards, at Gombroom, their home on North Fork, in 1890. This photograph may have been made at that time. Vance died in Washington, D.C., April 14, 1894. His body was returned to Asheville and placed in Riverside Cemetery. Vance had an illustrious career as a lawyer, congressman, soldier, governor, and senator. Vance monument on Pack Square and a monument in Raleigh were erected in his honor. Photograph from the North Carolina Collection, Pack Memorial Public Library.

On May 3, 1890, shortly after Senator and Mrs. Zebulon Vance had built Gombroom, their summer home at North Fork, they entertained for surviving members of Company F, Fourteenth North Carolina Regiment, Confederate Army, known as the Rough and Ready Guards. This was the unit organized and led by Vance until he became North Carolina's Civil War governor. Senator and Mrs. Vance are in the center. Surrounding them, left to right with feet on ground, William Gudger, of Azalea; Dr. David Gudger, Sand Hill; Capt. J. M. Gudger, Sr., Asheville; Guy Williams, Ivy; Billy Hunter, French Broad; Gen. Vic Baird, Reems Creek; Thomas Brooks, Candler, and Wesley Hicks, company cook from Asheville. On the first and second steps, James M. Smith, Asheville; William Garrison, Reems Creek; J. J. White, Swannanoa; Baechus Westall, Swannanoa; Judge Sam Cathey; J. M. (Jim) Green, Andy_____ , French Broad, and Alf Walton, Old Haw Creek road. In the back are John M. Stepp, Black Mountain; Jim Hughey, Bull Creek; Albert Lytle, Lower Cane Creek, Fairview; Riley Pitillo, Fairview; Percy Gaston, Sand Hill. Also present but not pictured were: Robert Williams, Fairview; George White, Bedent Smith, Reems Creek, and Thomas Johnston, Asheville. Information for this picture was supplied many years later by Judge Owen Gudger, local historian. Photograph courtesy of Frances McDowell.

As part of George Vanderbilt's eagerness to be part of the Asheville community, he asked architect Richard Sharp Smith to design a building to be known as the Young Mens Institute. The YMI building was built on Eagle Street in 1892 as a community center for black citizens. One of the first groups to organize in the center was the YMI Band, which became immediately popular for dances throughout the city. Photograph from the North Carolina Collection, Pack Memorial Public Library.

Visitors to Asheville could stay at the new Swannanoa Hotel on the left or the older Eagle Hotel on the right of South Main Street, now Biltmore Avenue. The streetcars at the top of the hill are at Public Square. Newspapers of the day editorialized against the tracks down the middle of Main Street because of the hazard created for a passing horse and buggy. In 1934 this street was widened by cutting back the stores on the east side (right side) of the street. The Eagle, which had been built in 1840 was removed. Photo courtesy of Jean Lance.

In 1891 when Charles D. Blanton was mayor of Asheville, the city received authority from the General Assembly to pass a bond issue of six hundred thousand dollars to pave the square and principal streets. Contractor P. M. B. Young used paving blocks to do Public Square. Photograph from the North Carolina Collection, Pack Memorial Public Library.

After an illustrious career as a statesman and soldier, Brig. Gen. Robert Brank Vance spent the last years of his life in this house on the west bank of the French Broad River near Alexander. Two years older than his brother Zebulon, General Vance came into prominence during the Civil War when he commanded forces in Western North Carolina and worked with Thomas' Legion, a Cherokee contingent, to build the Indian Gap road from Quallatown across the Smokies to Sevierville. Vance is reputed to have hauled cannons over the road in January 1864 to use them in defense of Western North Carolina. Following the war, Vance served in Congress, 1873 to 1885, was assistant to the commissioner of patents, 1885-89, and represented Buncombe County in Raleigh, 1894-96. His popularity in the county was shown when he spoke at the celebration of Buncombe's Centennial, August 11, 1892. The Asheville Daily Citizen reported, "General Vance was welcomed by the crowd with the fervor that is characteristic of a Buncombe audience when he appears." Photograph courtesy of the North Carolina Collection, Pack Memorial Public Library.

Bonniecrest Inn was typical of the hostelries that flourished in South Buncombe after the coming of the railroad in the 1880s. Others included Audubon Lodge, Mineral Springs Hotel, Sunset View, Arden House, Rosscragan Inn, and Busby Hall. Most, like Bonniecrest, had cottages on the grounds and offered sumptuous meals, nightly entertainment, and sports like tennis and horseback riding. Bonniecrest was owned by Mrs. Dora W. Doe, who became an innkeeper when her husband died, leaving her with three young children. Photograph courtesy of Virginia Ryman Morrison.

The train station at Skyland was built around 1895, thanks to the efforts of Otis A. Miller, an artist who came to the county from Minneapolis about 1886. This picture was made about 1900, as a Southern Railway steam train is pulling into the station. Photograph courtesy of Marion Case Havener.

Asheville's first government building and post office was erected in 1892 at the corner of Patton Avenue and Haywood Street on the triangle now known as Pritchard Park. Land for the building was donated by William Johnston, according to his descendants. In this view the left of the building including the tower is facing Patton Avenue. Back of the post office is what became Government Street, now College, and the rise of Battery Park Hill where Col. Frank Coxe had built his hotel in 1886. The first building on Government was the Medical Building, 1900, not showing here. Streetcar tracks are in place and the streets are paved with macadam, a process using layers of small stones rolled together with mud and perhaps tar or asphalt. Asheville Mayor Charles Blanton pushed for street paving and most major streets were macadamized by 1893. Photograph from the North Carolina Collection, Pack Memorial Public Library.

On March 4, 1893, the town of Black Mountain, formerly known as Grey Eagle, was chartered by the General Assembly of North Carolina. Town limits were to extend a mile in all directions from the railroad station, shown in the middle of this picture. Town limits had to be reduced to one-half mile, however, because the town couldn't provide services for a large hotel on Miami Mountain. T. K. Brown, the first mayor, served ten years. In 1910 when this picture was made Brown was paid one dollar a month as chief of police and G. W. Stepp was mayor. Photograph from the North Carolina Collection, Pack Memorial Public Library.

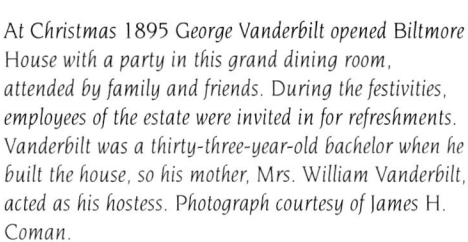

At Christmas 1895 George Vanderbilt opened Biltmore House with a party in this grand dining room, attended by family and friends. During the festivities, employees of the estate were invited in for refreshments. Vanderbilt was a thirty-three-year-old bachelor when he built the house, so his mother, Mrs. William Vanderbilt, acted as his hostess. Photograph courtesy of James H. Coman.

In 1896 this picture was made of cadets from Bingham Academy in parade on Public Square. Bingham was opened in 1891 by Col. Robert Bingham and operated until 1928. The school was located on the west side of the French Broad River near Richmond Hill. Photograph from the North Carolina Collection, Pack Memorial Public Library.

Ollie Hendricks was teacher for the children at Riceville School in 1897. The school, one of several founded by the Presbyterian church, was the first mission assignment for Frances Goodrich, famed Presbyterian missionary who later became the leader of the arts and crafts movement in the county. Goodrich came to Riceville in 1890 to assist Evangeline Godbold. Dr. Jan Davidson says in his introduction to a revised edition of Mountain Homespun that Goodrich's philosophy for helping mountain children was to set a model of good housekeeping and cleanliness and hope they would follow it. She and Godbold moved into their own cottage at Riceville and spent time visiting sick members of the Riceville Presbyterian Church. In 1892 they moved across the mountain to start a school and church at Brittain's Cove near Weaverville. Photograph courtesy of Ethel Austin.

Montreat, the Presbyterian retreat center north of Black Mountain, was started by the Mountain Retreat Association in 1897. Not only is it still a summer conference center for Presbyterians throughout the South, it is home for Montreat College. Hundreds of homes are on the Montreat grounds, many of which house retired Presbyterian missionaries. Photograph courtesy of the North Carolina Collection, Pack Memorial Public Library.

In this historic photograph of the laying of the cornerstone for the Vance Monument, Judge Walter E. Moore, grandmaster of the Masonic Lodge of the state of North Carolina, is making the principal address. After Vance's death the committee which had been formed to plan a suitable memorial ran into financial problems. George Pack asked the county for land at Public Square and volunteered to give two thousand dollars if the committee would raise the rest. Architect was Richard Sharp Smith; contractor, James G. Colvin. Ground was broken for the monument October 23, 1897, and the cornerstone laid December 22, 1897. The monument was completed March 11, 1898. Photograph courtesy of William Henry.

Many photographers have taken pictures of Asheville from Beaucatcher Mountain, as J. H. Tarbell did in 1897. Close examination shows many things: the courthouse filling the middle of Public Square, Battery Park Hotel high atop a hill, and what little development there was across the river. At the time this picture was taken, the county was in a financial crisis. From July to October three banks closed in downtown Asheville, all located around Public Square. Photograph courtesy of the North Carolina Collection, Pack Memorial Public Library.

The "Annual Festivities of the Jacob Weaver Family" convened at the home of its progenitor on Reems Creek Road in 1899. Jacob Weaver was a baby in 1787 when his parents, John and Elizabeth Biffle Weaver, carried him into the Reems Creek valley. The house pictured here, which is still standing, was originally a two-story log cabin built after Jacob was married to Elizabeth Siler in 1811. In the 1830s a frame part was added. The band on the second balcony was the Weaverville Brass Band, started by Capt. William Parker. Family meetings, often called reunions or decorations are a custom observed by many mountain families. Photograph courtesy of Josephine Osborne.

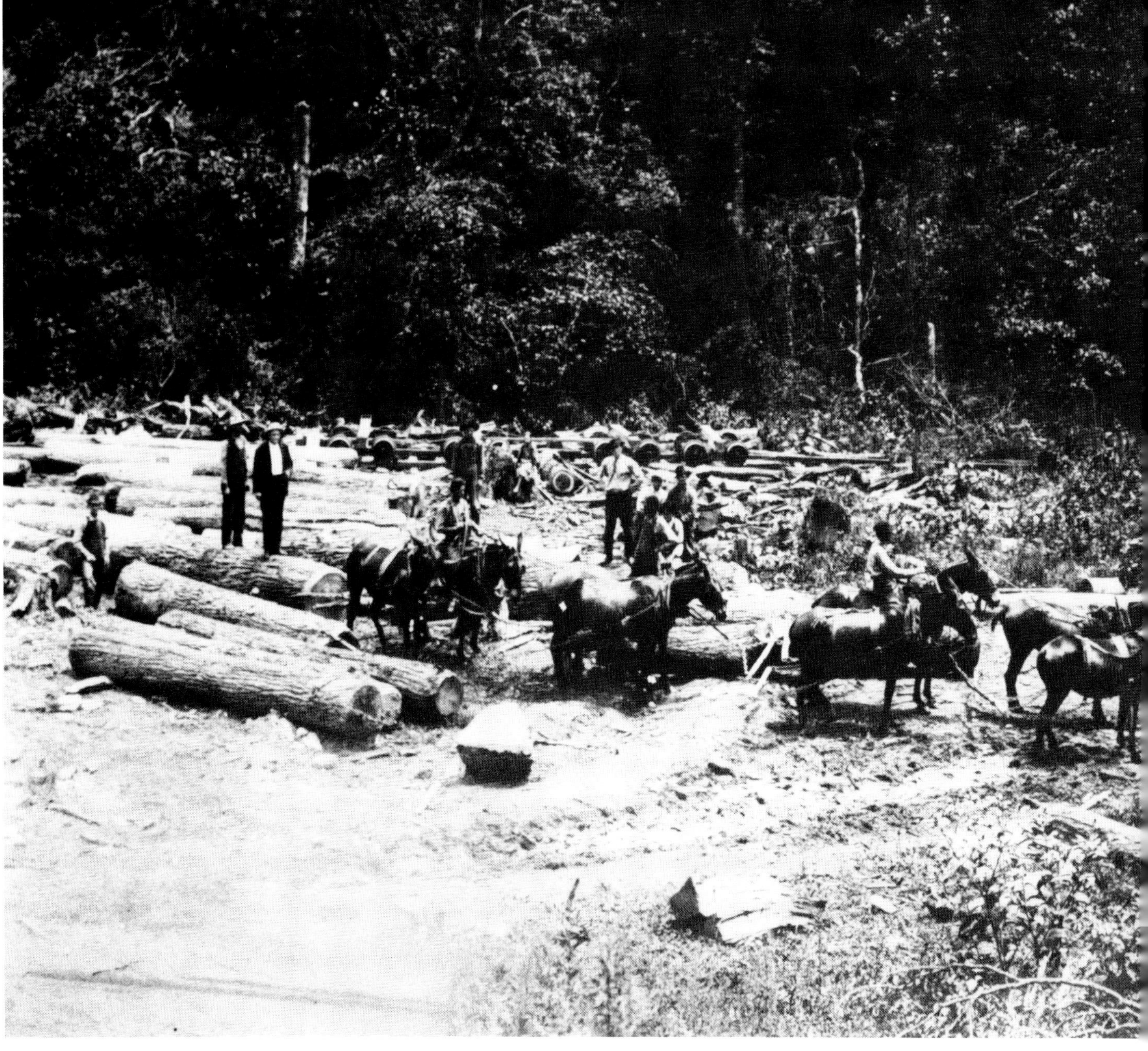

Men and Money
1900 to 1910

7

National attention focused on Buncombe and brought men with money and ideas. Edwin Wiley Grove bought Sunset Mountain and built the Grove Park Inn. His Grove Park Development provided suitable housing for the rich. Asheville School, Bingham Academy, and Christ School educated their sons.

Tourists from hotter climates flocked to inns in outlying communities. Some brought families and baggage and stayed all summer. It became hard to tell a hotel or a boarding house from a sanitarium as the cooler, fresher air of the mountains continued to draw those with respiratory ailments.

Population of the county in the census of 1910 was 49,798, with more than half from rural areas. Awareness of the living conditions of mountain people began to surface. Social programs were begun.

The international market for arts and crafts made an impact on mountain craftmen. Better roads programs found a cause. Of the 177 school districts in the city and county, 103 had schoolhouses in 1905. Of those, 95 were one-room schools. First grade teachers were paid thirty dollars a month.

The word "conservation" was well-known to lumbermen in Buncombe County by the turn of the century, thanks to the school of forestry started in Pisgah by Carl Schenck and the initiatives taken by Dr. George Ambler in Asheville to have a federal forestry program. There was little practice of it, however. It was as though trees were an inexhaustible resource. In locations where a steam boiler could be dragged into the woods, sawmills were set up. Where a small engine could be used, trees were shipped out on a narrow-gauge road or along an already cut road. But, where the going was tough or steep, mules were chained to the logs which had to be skinned out. If small trees or undergrowth got in the way, those plants became victims. The first acts which enabled the secretary of agriculture to buy land in Western North Carolina was passed in 1901, with the assistance of Sen. Jeter Pritchard of North Carolina. Pisgah National Forest was created by proclamation issued by President Woodrow Wilson on October 17, 1916. By proclamation on July 13, 1936, President Franklin D. Roosevelt established the boundaries of Pisgah with 1,178,003 acres. Pisgah Forest, with headquarters in Asheville, covers national forest land in several counties. Photographs from the North Carolina Collection, Pack Memorial Public Library.

Settlers began moving into the Sandy Mush Valley about 1800 and the Big Sandy Methodist Episcopal Church South was built in 1837 on land deeded to the trustees by Jeper and David Palmer. The first building, built of large bricks made locally, housed the church and a school known as the Brick Church School. The frame building shown which houses the Sandy Mush United Methodist Church was built by Will E. Waldrop and Will Duckett in 1904. In the Asheville Citizen of 1892 A. C. Robeson tells how Sandy Mush Creek got its name. Robeson said early explorers, Strawther and his crew, were camped beside the creek. While dipping water to cook mush they scooped up some sand; hence the name. A Mr. King cut the first clearing in the valley with the help of a black man. It was located a few hundred yards above the church site. Photograph courtesy of James H. Coman.

Fairview Inn was built as a home by Jason Ashworth in about 1880. Around 1900 Thomas Long added a dining room and ten cottages and operated the inn. From 1934 to 1939 Herman and Virginia Kennickell were the innkeepers. The inn closed after World War II. Photograph courtesy of Virginia Williams Kennickell.

Ben Williams was storekeeper in the village of Fairview for forty years, handling everything from groceries, to domestics, to shoes. Everett Ledbetter said when he bought the store in 1939, it took him months to sell out the mercantile side and turn it into a grocery store. Photograph courtesy of Mr. and Mrs. Everett Ledbetter.

Hominy station, located on Southern lines west of Asheville, was a typical local station in 1900. Stations like this were used frequently by farmers and others who lived in the county for transportation to town. Also, when goods were needed from Asheville, they were shipped on the train. Photograph courtesy of Richard Gudger.

Carson School opened on Haw Branch in Big Ivy community about 1902. When school busses transported the children to the new Barnardsville School, Harris Dillingham moved the building and called it Carson Store. This little building is gone now, but a replica is planned in celebration of the Buncombe County Bicentennial in 1992. The Big Ivy Community Club will oversee the reconstruction of the little school on community club property. Photograph courtesy of Big Ivy Community Club.

When the land for Brown's Chapel Missionary Baptist Church was given by James and Nancy Sawyer, John and Julie Holcombe, and R. M. and Harriet Holcombe, the donors stipulated that "the ceiling, seats, and doors shall be put in by June 1, 1901. The belfry, bell and blinds be put in by June 1, 1902 which will complete the building for all intents and purposes." The church was named for an early pastor, the Reverend Thomas K. Brown, father of former sheriff Lawrence Brown. The congregation built a new building in 1954. Photograph courtesy of "Pat" Rhea Hensley.

In 1904 the county school board paid W. H. Lord ten dollars to prepare plans and specifications for six new "school houses." Builder J. R. Herren was paid $583.00 to build this new Swannanoa school. In 1925 when the school burned, boys from the high school were called out to form a bucket brigade from the Swannanoa River. The story is that they poured the water on the ground, because the school was so out-of-date. Photograph courtesy of the Valley Museum, Black Mountain.

Like John the Baptist in the River Jordan, many early preachers baptized in cold mountain streams. The history of Hominy Baptist Church, written in 1987 for the 175th anniversary describes a baptism in Hominy Creek in 1907. "No pentecostal tongues of fire, no rushing winds, just the constant sound of the creek and the voice of the preacher and the people." Photograph from the North Carolina Collection, Pack Memorial Public Library.

Manning Lance farmed on Bent Creek until he sold the land to George Vanderbilt in 1902. The land had been part of a 1824 land grant to Abraham Runnels. In a paper on the history of early settlement and land use on the Bent Creek Experimental Forest, William A. Nesbitt tells a story about the Manning land. In one summer forty head of cattle had died there from what local people called "milk sickness." They believed the malady rose from mineral deposits in the earth and settled with the dew on plants which the cattle ate. An old-timer named Pink Jones drank water from a spring on the same area. Pink developed "milk sickness" and nearly died, so, to this day, many local residents refuse to drink water from that spring. After he sold the land to Vanderbilt, Lance moved his family to a two-story house at the intersection of Monte Vista Road and Brooks Cove Road. Photograph courtesy of Doris Lance Plemmons.

Former Chairman of the County Commissioners Coke Candler was a little boy when he attended Glady Fork School, circa 1903, in South Hominy but in later years he put his name on this picture. Candler is the child in front. The teacher was Miss Lillie Candler. The young man leaning against the school to the left was Milton Roberson, whose job was to drive Miss Lillie to school in a buggy. Photograph courtesy of Sara Roberson Long.

Each individual has his own history, but the history that gives him roots is his connection with his ancestors, their parcel of land, and often the house in which they lived. The family of Robert Weaver is a good example. In the rocking chair is Julia Coulter Weaver, who was about eighty when this picture was made on the porch of the Jacob Weaver home. Julia and her husband Jesse Richardson Weaver had given up their own home and returned here when Jesse's mother Elizabeth Siler Weaver (Mrs. Jacob) became ill. History had repeated itself for at the time this photo was taken, circa 1903, Robert had returned to be with Julia. With Robert Henry and his wife Martha Webb Weaver are, first row, left to right, Lucius, Glen, Lucy, and Pearl. Second row, Agnes on Martha's lap and Caroline by her grandmother. Third row, Minnie and Hattie Culbreath who lived with the family and is buried in the Weaver family cemetery. One of the girls was asked how many children were in their family. Her reply, "Seven white 'uns and one black." Photograph courtesy of Dry Ridge Museum, Weaverville.

Mountain Meadows Inn stood for almost fifty years at Peach Knob on what became Elk Mountain Road. Built after George Douglas Miller bought the land from William F. Rice in 1902, the inn opened only in the summer months. It catered to a distinguished clientele and provided employment to young people of the area, who waited tables, cleaned, cooked, or tended the horses. Three of the men holding horses, Ernest Ray, Kelly Shope, and Luther Ray, brought guests to the inn via a forest road from Riceville Road. Photographs courtesy of Ethel Austin.

After an outstanding career as a designer and building of tile structures, Raphael Guastivino retired to a home in Black Mountain and turned his attentions to making wine and other pursuits. When he told his priest that he was going to build a chapel on his property, the parishioners of St. Lawrence Catholic Church in Asheville convinced him to build it in town instead. Guastivino died in 1908 while he was finishing St. Lawrence. His son had a chapel built in his memory and he is buried there. Guastivino's tile work has taken on new importance as more students are doing research about the man and studying his designs. He was a renowned designer and builder of arches, domes, and other structures reminiscent of Moorish Spain. George Vanderbilt brought him to Asheville to work in the Biltmore House. Photograph courtesy of the Valley Museum, Black Mountain.

87

For vacationers and those attending Presbyterian meetings, Alba Hotel was built at Montreat in 1906 on the banks of Lake Susan. When it burned in 1945, it was replaced with Montreat Inn, a multi-story rock building. Photograph courtesy of the North Carolina Collection, Pack Memorial Public Library.

Ridgecrest, known as Blue Monte, came into prominence as a tourist destination for stagecoaches. A toll booth at the top of the ridge charged five cents for those riding horseback through the Swannanoa Gap, ten cents for carriages and wagons. When the Western North Carolina Railroad was being built in 1879, the community was renamed Terrell's Station and became a rollicking way-station for the workers with dormitories, saloons, working girls, and other comforts. Today Ridgecrest is prominent as the eastern assembly grounds of the Southern Baptist Convention. This photo, taken shortly after its opening in 1908, is of old Pritchard Hall at the assembly grounds. Photograph courtesy of the Valley Museum, Black Mountain.

The first wedding to be held in the present building of Grace Episcopal Church on Merrimon Avenue was conducted about 1907 by the Reverend William Francis Rice. The Reverend Mr. Rapp was married to a Miss Russell, shown on the church steps. The Reverend Rice served the church from the time it became an organized mission of the Diocese of North Carolina in 1881 until he retired in 1907. Richard Sharp Smith was architect of Grace Episcopal Church. Photograph courtesy of Frank Roberson.

Before the Civil War, Asheville constructed a reservoir "not far north of the western end of Beaucatcher Tunnel," according to Sondley's history, and dug a trench to carry a water pipe toward Public Square. Because of the war, however, it was 1884 before the reservoir and pipelines were put into use. Col. T. W. Patton suggested pumping water into it from streams northwest of the gap. In 1886 the old reservoir was tied into a pumping station on the Swannanoa River near what is now Recreation Park. The reservoir was used again in 1902 and 1903 when the city piped water from the North Fork watershed. Finally, in 1907 the city built a new reservoir on Beaucatcher a little north of Beaucatcher Gap. That reservoir is probably the one in the top center of this picture. On the hill to the right is the home of J. Evans Brown, completed in 1889 and called Zealandia. Brown lived in the house until his death in 1895. The gap shown with an old road crossing it is where Beaucatcher Cut pierced the mountain in the early 1980s. Photograph courtesy of the North Carolina Collection, Pack Memorial Public Library.

89

Following a successful vote in North Carolina for the prohibition of alcohol in 1908, the forces that had worked in the campaign celebrated by holding a rally on the Haywood Street bridge and dumping the contents of beer barrels and whiskey bottles into the French Broad. For others, however, the decision was not a happy one. Some prominent citizens announced that they were going back to the north. Photograph courtesy of Francis McDowell.

Credit for the success of many Buncombe County students in the early days goes to the abilities of the teachers, certainly not to the facilities. Cash Roberson, pictured here with sixth and seventh grade students from Candler High School, circa 1910, was one of those teachers. With Roberson in front are Harry Gudger and Doyce Clark. Second row, left to right are: George Malonee, Debbie Williams, Lucinda Candler, Charity Williams, Mildred Hyatt, Margarite Taylor, Margaret Powell, Mary Ledford, Mary Powell, and T. A. Groce. In the third row are: Mary Brannon, Sallie Penland, Edna Cathey, Florence Cathey, Charles DeBrew, Ralph Hipps, Alton Hall, Avery Jamison, and Dock Cole. In the fourth row are: Pansy Rutherford, Sadie Howard, Charlotte Cathey, Coke Candler, Corrie Lee Howell, Dorothy Whiteside, Margaret Whiteside, and Helen Penland. In the fifth row are: Harry Sellers, George Cathey, Pat Howell, and Wayne Morgan. Photograph courtesy of Sara Roberson Long.

A placid scene of Kenilworth in the snow is not the right picture to illustrate the obsession Jake Chiles had for creating the development. The fire that destroyed Kenilworth Inn in 1908 set his direction. Not only did Chiles buy the inn, he rebuilt it with the help of investors and laid out a complete town, including a lake. He even visited Kenilworth Castle in England to see where the name came from. Chiles died of a heart attack at age thirty-five, leaving a wife and two small children. Leah Arcouet Chiles, mayor of Kenilworth when the city wanted to annex it, would not consent to annexation without a vote of the residents. By one vote Kenilworth became part of Asheville, June 30, 1929. Photograph from the North Carolina Collection, Pack Memorial Public Library.

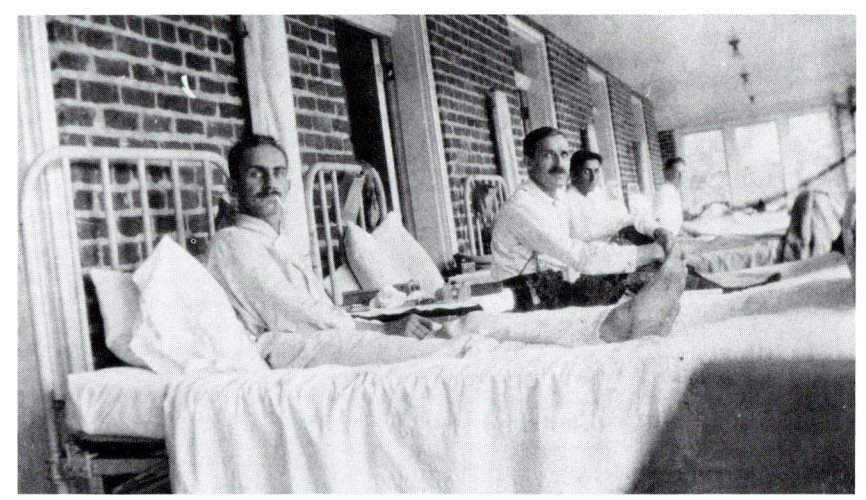

The attitude of the people of Buncombe County toward tubercular patients who came by the hundreds was not always favorable. Dr. Irby Stephens in an article written for the North Carolina Medical Journal said this bad feeling may have caused one of the first tuberculosis specialists, Dr. Joseph W. Gleitsmann, to leave in 1882. At that time tuberculosis was a dreaded disease, the leading cause of death in the United States. Dr. Gleitsmann felt the combination of altitude and climate found in Asheville promoted a cure. These men are pictured on the porch of St. Joseph's Sanitarium after it moved to its location on Biltmore Avenue. The success of their treatment depended on their sleeping in the fresh air, regardless of the temperature. Photograph from the album of Ella Case. Photograph courtesy of Marion Case Havener.

Fairview Academy, or Fairview Collegiate Institute as it was known later, was a private boarding school, opened in 1888, at a time when most communities didn't have a high school. Professor W. A. G. Brown was first principal. Students paid a regular tuition fee, but the boys cut wood and built fires while the girls swept and helped with the cooking. Parents often furnished wood or produce in return for tuition. These pictures, circa 1909, show the size of the student body, many of whom came from surrounding counties. In the high school were, first row left to right, Grace McAbee, Flora Henderson, Edna Reed, Kate Jones, Lillian Miller, Rollie Pitillo, and Nanie Ashworth. Second row, Fred Lyda, Portia Freeman, Mallie Williams, Ella Lyda, ____Williams, Laura Smart, and Mattie Smart. Third row, teacher Irene Abernathy, Bonnie Shuford, Bob Jones, ____Gilliam, Julia Wilson, Mac Jones, Julia Vehorn, Minnie Bass, and teacher Edna Lynch. Fourth row, Claude Ashworth, Elsie Ashworth, Carl Merrill, Albert Bright, and H. F. Hunter, principal. Photograph courtesy of Virginia Williams Kennickell.

With the coming of the railroad to Black Mountain in 1879, the small community tasted the prosperity that comes from being a tourist mecca. In 1910 photographer H. W. Pelton was commissioned to do postcards for two imposing-looking hostelries. The Black Mountain Inn was erected by Mayor T. K. Brown as a residence. A. E. Stevens converted it into a hotel in 1898. The Gladstone was opened in 1902 by Manley and Bell of Mount Olive. Its name was later changed to the Gresham. Photographs from the North Carolina Collection, Pack Memorial Public Library.

William Sidney Porter, who wrote under the pen name O'Henry was married to Sara Coleman of Weaverville about 1900. He moved to Weaverville and opened an office downtown but New York drew him back. He died there in 1910 and was returned to Asheville where he was buried in Riverside Cemetery. Photograph from the North Carolina Collection, Pack Memorial Public Library.

"Uncle Dave" Penland brought a bouquet of moss and wild flowers to the Beech Community Fourth of July celebration each year. The ladies looked forward to his coming, because he picked one of them to give it to. With Penland and his bouquet, circa 1910, are Sara Lewis Penland and a Mrs. Brown. Photograph courtesy of "Pat" Rhea Hensley.

Jamie Owen lived in a log cabin in Chunns Cove. Very faithful to her church, she was well known to the parishioners of St. Luke Episcopal Church. Her livelihood came from the sale of milk from a small dairy herd. Before the milk law was passed in the 1960s that required milkers to use refrigerated tanks, the small farmer would set milk out in cans to be picked up each morning by the dairymen. Photograph courtesy of Eugenia Ray Carter.

Floods, War, and Women's Rights

1910 to 1920

All seemed "peachy keen" on the domestic front in 1910—industry, new hotels, new jobs, more transportation, and prosperity just around the corner.

There were rumblings in Europe, but no one thought America would be drawn into the war. There was talk, too, from the women about the vote and from the school board about new high schools. School districts passed more than a half million in sinking fund bonds for school construction. From 1916 to 1930 thirty-two buildings were constructed.

No one figured on the flood of 1916. It was unthinkable that it could rain enough to run the Swannanoa and French Broad rivers and all the county streams out of their banks.

Everyone cheered World War I when it came. The marching units held parades downtown. Everyone grew extra food to send to the soldiers. The men marched off to France with the Thirtieth Division.

Strangest of all was the vote for the women. Ratified in August of 1920, the vote gave women new power and they sent a woman off to Raleigh to represent the county.

After serving in the United States Army in the Spanish American War, E. W. Pearson moved to Asheville in 1906. On Labor Day, 1912 he introduced a new subdivision for West Asheville which included a park called Pearson Park. The first Buncombe County District Agricultural Fair was held at Pearson Park in 1914 and in 1916 the first black baseball team in Asheville began playing there. Photograph courtesy of Iola Pearson Byers.

Turkey Creek Baptist Church, founded in 1858, served as both church and school for many years. These children, circa 1912, attended school for four months, grades one through eight with one teacher. Pictured are, front row, left to right, Pauline Brown, Roy Brown, Mark Plemmons, Plummen Lowe, Erskine Plemmons, Davie Martin, Rena Lowe Henderson, Mae Plemmons, and Cancel Brown. Back row, teacher Tennie Brown, Strobic Hawkins Davis, Irene Brown, Elsie Martin Bradley, Faraday Snelson, Hyleman Plemmons, Nora Lowe, Sewell Brown, James Plemmons, Howard Plemmons, Esse Vaughn, Mark Plemmons, and Walter Webb. In the 1920s this building was replaced with the present church building and the children went to a consolidated school in Leicester. Photo courtesy of the Reverend Erskine Plemmons.

Robert E. Lee Hall, 1911, was the first building erected on the grounds of the Blue Ridge Assembly near Black Mountain. In 1903 the Blue Ridge Association bought land that had originally belonged to Maj. John Dougherty. The first conference at Blue Ridge was held in 1913. Dr. W. D. Weatherford was elected executive secretary, a post he held for many years. Lee School for Boys met in Robert E. Lee Hall for four years, from 1926 to 1930. Today over fifty buildings cover the fifteen-hundred-acre assembly grounds. They accommodate visitors to a year-round schedule of conferences. Photograph by William A. Barnhill. Used courtesy North Carolina Collection, Pack Memorial Public Library.

Penland Stone Pottery at Jugtown near Candler produced hand-turned utility stoneware. This pottery was one of the many in the county that used native clay. The potter is unknown, but the look on his face shows his intensity as he turned a crock on a wheel controlled by a foot pedal. Photograph courtesy of James H. Coman.

Evidence of the fun and popularity of Montreat Assembly is shown in this wonderful old photo of Stunt Day at Montreat in 1912. The dam burst and the lake washed away in the flood of 1916, but it has been built back and today is known as Lake Susan. Photograph courtesy of the North Carolina Collection, Pack Memorial Public Library.

By 1917 Riceville School had new facilities. In that year Buncome County began to realize it had serious problems in education and school districts began to take a look at themselves. One district report is quoted in Leonard Miller's book, "Two items of livestock were of special interest: The total absence of sheep and the presence of thirty-four dogs. We wonder if there is any connection? We hold no brief against the dogs; but it was entertaining at least, to us as teachers, to ascertain that to feed the dogs, estimating the cost at ten cents a day per dog, costs the community almost exactly five times as much as is being put into the education of the children of the community." Photograph courtesy of the Valley Museum, Black Mountain.

James S. Rhea of Beech community and his son Leonard entered the corn piled in their farmyard in a county-wide contest sponsored by the Corn Club about 1918. Prior to 4H Clubs, young men joined Corn Clubs and young women Tomato Clubs. Corn was shucked and left in a pile until the agent could come by. Then it was measured. The young man growing the largest number of bushels per acre was winner. Photograph courtesy of "Pat" Rhea Hensley.

When the thrashing machine replaced the hand sickle, crews of men with a machine moved from farm to farm to cut hay or grain. The work sometimes took several days. While the crew was there the farmer's wife could call in relatives and neighbors to cook a good noon meal for the men. Photograph courtesy of Mabel Duckett.

An artist with a camera, William A. Barnhill roamed Buncombe county for more than seventy years taking pictures that would typify folk life. He was particularly interested in the handicrafts and music. Barnhill found many subjects for his pictures, for he was in Buncombe County during the era when men and women still remembered and practiced the ways of their ancestors. This picture of Barnhill was made in 1915 in the Beech community. Photograph courtesy of Martha Barnhill Homer.

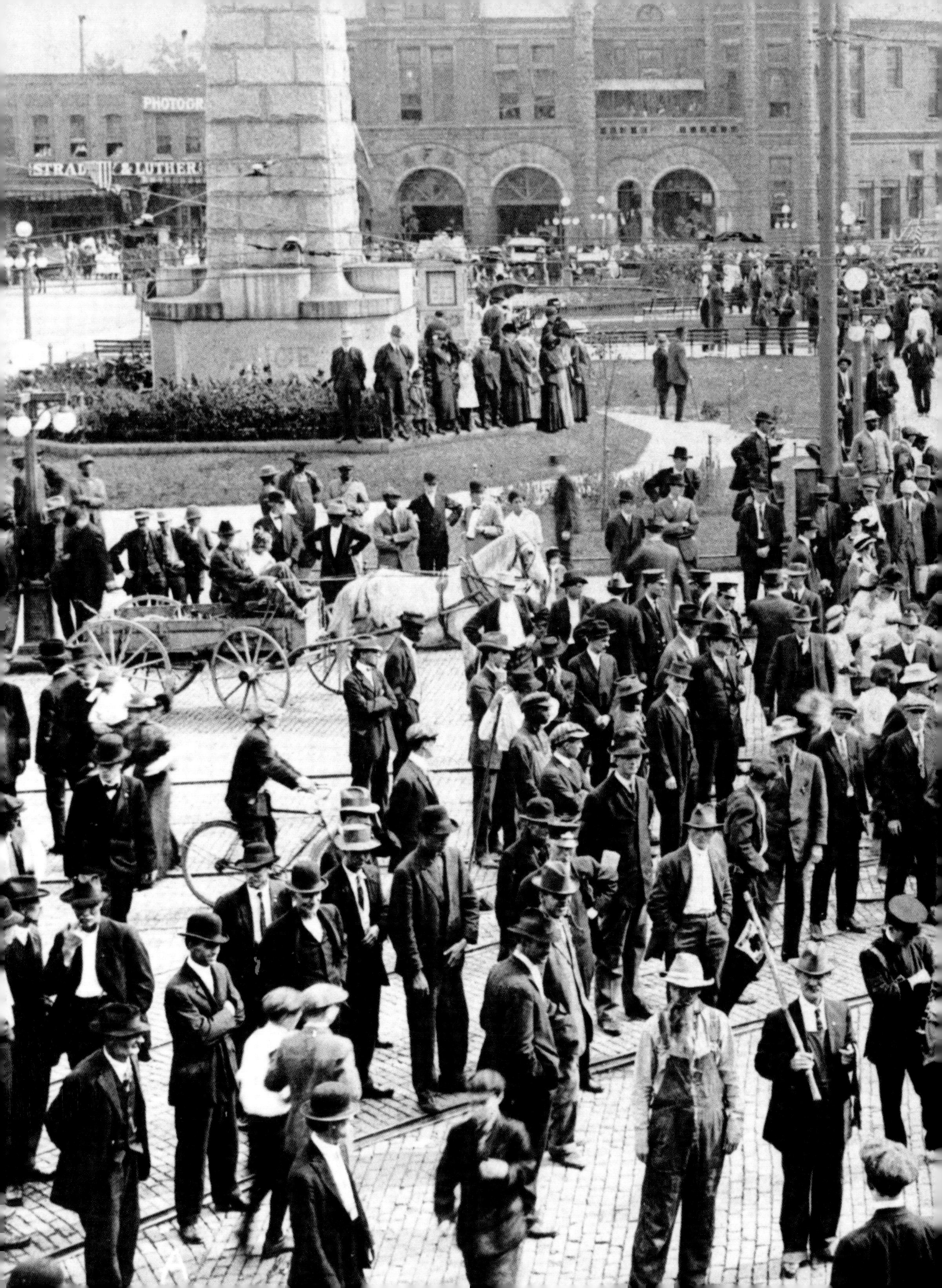
PHOTOGR
STRAD
& LUTHER

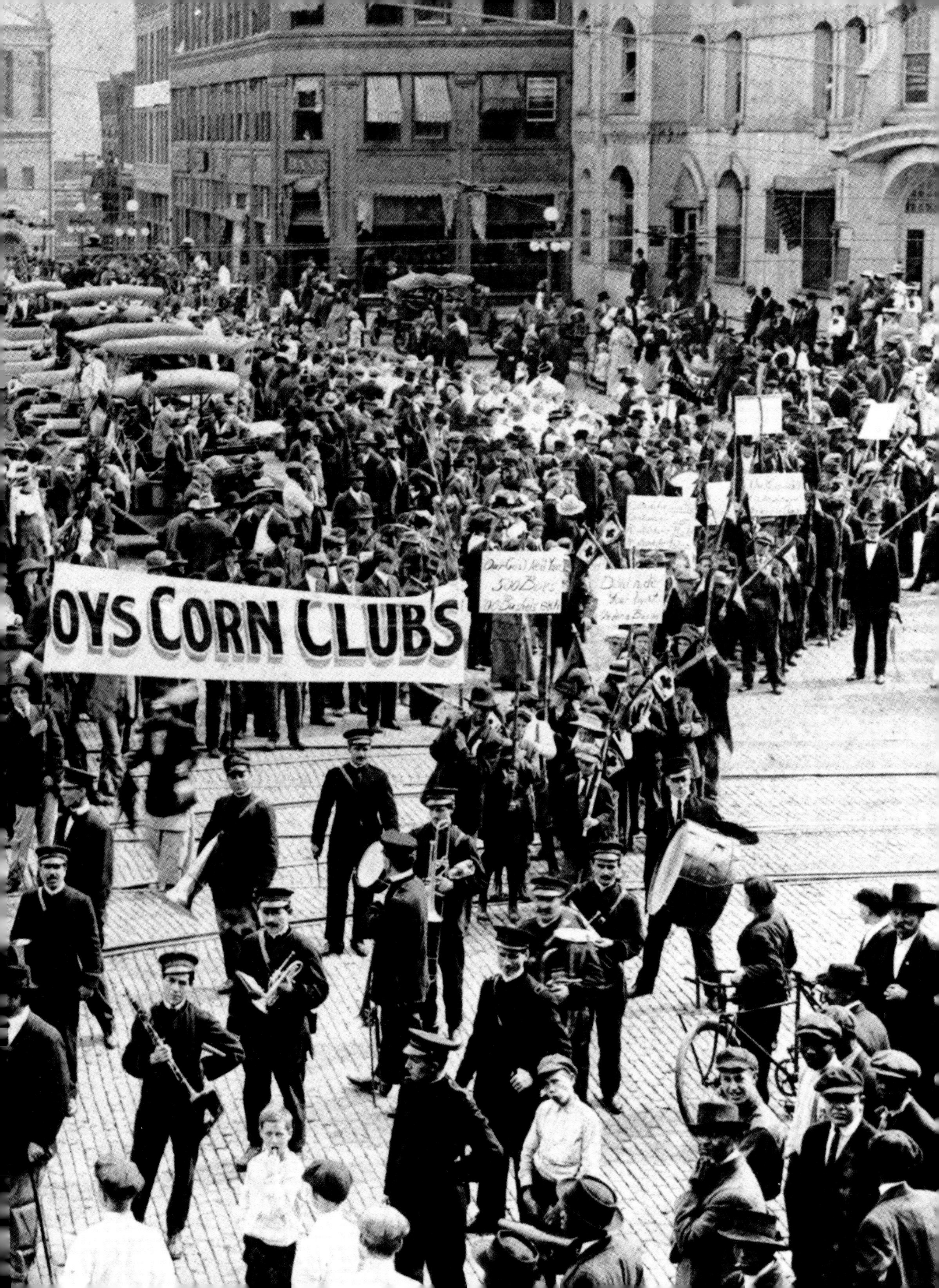
OYS CORN CLUBS

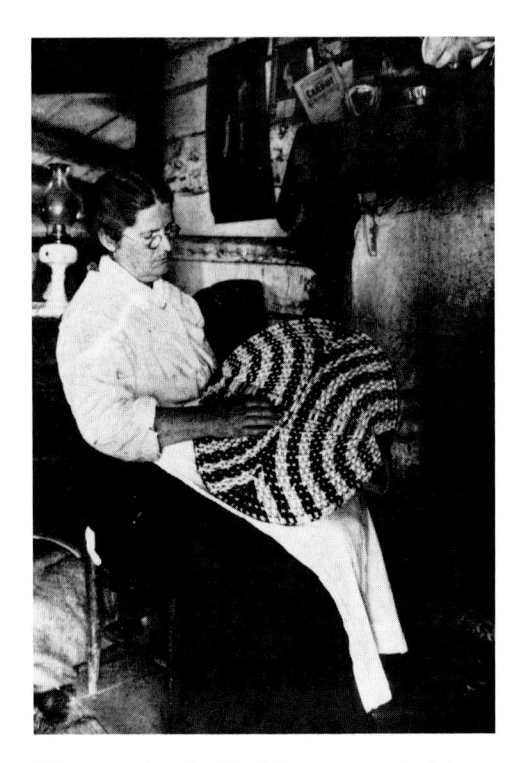

Using a maul made of the hub of a wagon wheel, Mr. Littrell of Skyland carefully cut white oak splits with which his wife made baskets. The splits were cut from small white oak saplings, especially gathered for that purpose. Mrs. Littrell would dye the saplings with colors made by boiling native plants. Then, she soaked them to make them more pliable. Picture by William A. Barnhill, from the North Carolina Collection, Pack Memorial Public Library.

Previous spread: The Corn Club was something to celebrate at the end of World War I, so they organized a parade on Pack Square. Farm Demonstration agent Ethan Douglas Weaver led the group. Boys from all over the county competed. Winner was Thomas Crawford Roberson, a sophomore in Candler High School. For raising one hundred forty-nine bushels and two pounds, Roberson's prize was a corn sheller and twenty-five dollars in cash. Photograph from the Dry Ridge Museum, Weaverville.

Bark baskets were the trade of Confederate veteran Dave Penland. These baskets like the one slung over his chair were made of dried bark carefully removed from saplings and curved over a mold. Penland used leather thongs or wood splints to lash the bark together and make a basket suitable for berry picking. Photograph by William H. Barnhill, from the North Carolilna Collection, Pack Memorial Public Library.

The Barnardsville district issued long-term sinking fund bonds for six thousand dollars in 1916 to finance a brick school building. Prior to that time children attended school in the frame building shown here. At the new school Sam R. White was principal. One of his teachers was F. A. Penland who later became principal at Weaverville. Photographs courtesy of Big Ivy Community Club, Barnardsville.

Wilbur Armstrong and his brother John were dairymen who ran the Oak Grove Farm on eighty-five acres in Chunns Cove. The Armstrongs delivered milk, butter, cheese, and eggs, in this horse-pulled cart. In the summer, in particular, dairymen had a booming business with deliveries to the many hotels and boarding houses in the county. Photograph courtesy of Eugenia Ray Carter.

Out toward Skyland W. A. Barnhill found Mr. Earwood, mountain fiddler. The violin, or fiddle as it was more commonly called, came from the old country with the Scotch-Irish settlers. It, and the banjo brought by the black people from Africa, were the favorite instruments to play for square dancing. A good fiddler was always popular at corn huskings or weddings. Photograph from the North Carolina Collection, Pack Memorial Public Library.

The Royal Giants, Asheville's first black baseball team, celebrated July Fourth, 1916, with a game at Pearson's Park in West Asheville. The man in the straw hat is E. W. Pearson who built the park. It was located at the intersection of Fayetteville and Ohio streets. Photograph courtesy of Iola P. Byers.

In about 1914 Walter B. Stephens set up a pottery with C. P. Ryman in Skyland and began making the matt glazed, hand decorated pottery which he labeled Nonconnah. In 1916 the chairman of art for the North Carolina Federation of Women's Clubs, Mrs. Jacques Busbee, wrote about his work, "The kiln at Skyland is very interesting....doing work that resembles Wedgewood. He is experimenting with more intelligence than anyone in the State." In 1926 Stephens owned Pisgah Pottery on Brevard Road. There he developed highfire vitrified ware which he signed and dated. Photograph courtesy of Virginia Ryman Morrison.

Mighty chestnut trees filled the forests of Western North Carolina until 1915 when a blight caused them to die. United States Forest Service personnel have struggled to overcome the scourge, but to no avail. Small trees grow to be about twenty feet before they become victims of the lingering blight. Photograph courtesy of Bent Creek Research and Demonstration Forest.

Tragedy struck Riverside Park twice in as many years. In 1915 a major part of the park burned; in 1916 the French Broad River flooded and washed out the lake. Thus, a major investment made by Asheville Electric Company in 1904 was no more. Asheville had lost a playground. In this panoramic view of the park Richmond Pearson's residence Richmond Hill in its original location shows well in the background. Pearson also suffered a set-back with the flood when the iron bridge across the river to his property washed away. The bridge was rebuilt, but not in the same location. Photograph from the North Carolina Collection, Pack Memorial Public Library.

St. Joseph's Hospital on Biltmore Avenue grew in spurts. In 1900 three nuns from Belmont Abbey opened St. Joseph's Retreat on French Broad Avenue to help those suffering from tuberculosis. After a move to Starnes Avenue, St. Joseph Sanitarium settled on Biltmore Avenue in 1909 in a house formerly occupied by W. W. McDowell and family. The sanitarium changed to a general hospital in 1916 and the Sisters of Mercy began closing in sleeping porches. The south wing was built in 1917, the administration area and the north wing 1924. The Depression and World War II slowed building, so it was 1952 before Loretta Hall for nurses could be built and 1958 before the Madonna Wing opened. These buildings were replaced with a ten-story, ultra-modern, regional care facility in 1974. Photograph by Bob Lindsey, courtesy of James H. Coman.

Schooling had been so sporadic in the County that by 1917 there were a great number of illiterate adults. To remedy the problem the school board hired Laura M. Jones to begin a program of adult education. When Elizabeth C. Morriss became supervisor in 1919 the community schools as they were called became the focus of both city and county. The slogan adopted was "A parent taught means a child in school." Many adult classes were taught at night as shown in this picture made at Sandy Mush School. Photograph courtesy of the North Carolina Collection, Pack Memorial Public Library.

Oates Field on Southside Avenue was a major playing area for black baseball teams. In 1918 the semi-professional team Royal Giants challenged a team from Greenville, South Carolina, at Oates Field. After the ballpark at Riverside Park washed away in the flood of 1916, this park served all Asheville teams until McCormick field was built. Photograph courtesy of Iola P. Byers.

The building of Azalea Veterans Hospital at Oteen in 1918 necessitated more transportation for that area, so a group of local men opened a bus line. Owners were Martin L. Ray, Johnny Matthews, and Bobby Hall. Ray also operated a taxi company. Photograph courtesy of Eugenia Ray Carter.

In World War I, the Thirtieth Division was made up of men from North Carolina, Tennessee, and Georgia, included a large number of men from Buncombe County. The division, known as Old Hickory, is credited with having smashed the Hindenberg Line. In 1919 men of Old Hickory held a reunion in Asheville. The unit remained together as part of the National Guard until World War II, when it took on men from other states, landed at Normandy, and made a significant difference in Europe for a second time. Photograph courtesy of the Smith McDowell House.

Distinctive white barns and silos on the hillside across from American Enka stood as a landmark until the 1970s, but the unusual dairy operation run there by Hans Pondoppidan, known as Hans Broby, had been closed for many years. During World War I Broby was manager of Carolina Creamery on Patton Avenue while owner Curtis Bynum was in France. An opportunity to supply milk for the new tubercular hospital at Oteen came up. With the encouragement of Mrs. Bynum, Broby bought additional cows and expanded the business to take care of the demand. When he returned, Bynum was so grateful to Broby for his initiative he set him up in business at Valkyrie in 1920. Broby was Danish, the son of Hendrik Pondoppidan, a Nobel Prize winner for literature. For the dairy he used methods learned in the old country. Instead of pasteurizing the milk, he sanitized the facility, even dressed the workers in white. When Broby died, he was buried in the Bynum family plot at Calvary Episcopal Church in Fletcher. Valkyrie and the Carolina Creamery were purchased by Sealtest Dairy. Photograph courtesy of Eleanor N. Rice.

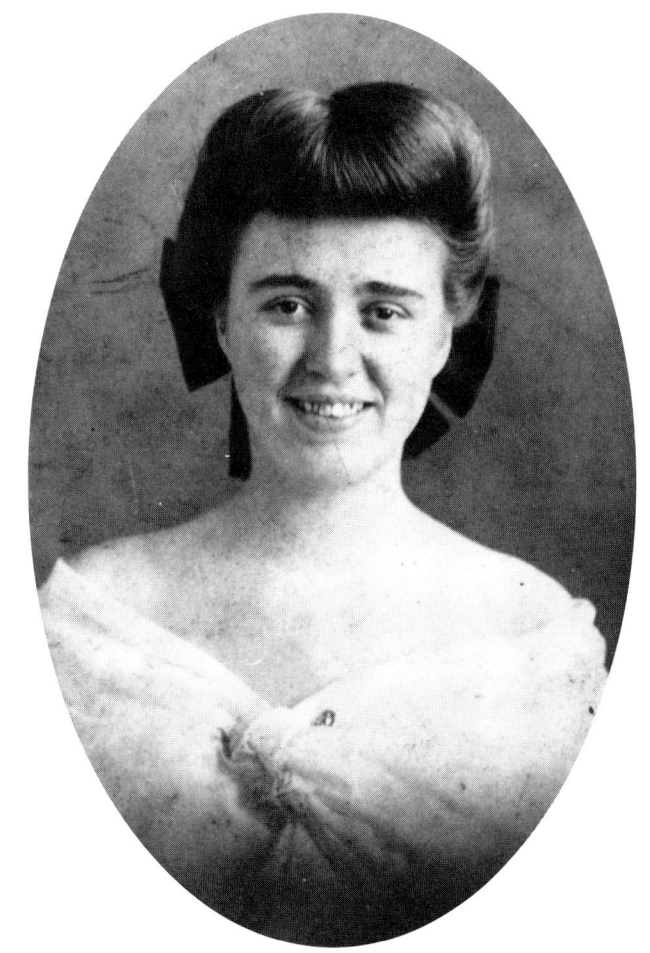

After the turn of the century an industrial development on the French Broad in Woodfin brought the National Casket Plant to the county. In this picture, made by Plateau Studios in 1920, Riverside Road is shown as it passed the plant. Land on which the plant was built had been the home-site of Zebulon Baird. N. A. Woodfin owned this property after the Civil War and the development was named for him. Part of this plant has been taken down. The remaining buildings are shared by Silverline Plastics and Malta Window Center. Photograph from the Southern Highlands Research Center, University of North Carolina at Asheville.

Exum Clement, known as "Brother Exum" to her fellow legislators, was the first woman to serve in the North Carolina House of Representatives. She was practicing law in Asheville in 1920 when she ran for the state office and won by a landslide. Born in the North Fork Community, Clement began school in a one-room school in Black Mountain, attended Normal and Collegiate Institute and Asheville Business College. She read for the law under J. J. Britt and Robert C. Goldstein. Bills introduced by Clement in the legislature included the unification of state and county for forest conservation, a pure milk bill calling for tuberculin testing for cows, a bill for private voting booths, help for abandoned wives, and approval in Buncombe for a home for unwed mothers. When she spoke on the latter in Asheville, her fellow citizens bombarded her with eggs and vegetables. Clement retired from public life after she was married to Eller E. Stafford. Photograph courtesy of Stafford Anders.

Asheville's professional baseball team has been called the Tourists since 1919 and has played in McCormick Field since 1924. A new ball park is planned for the 1992 season. Losing McCormick Field will be the passing of an era for many fans who, except for a few years during the Depression and World War II, have watched professional ball on the old field since the 1920s. Selected scenes for the movie Bull Durham were shot at McCormick Field. Photograph from the North Carolina Collection, Pack Memorial Public Library.

Boom and Bust

1920 to 1930

9

The mania known as the boom affected Buncombe County as it did the city. Water lines ran up Beaucatcher, Town Mountain, and Elk Mountain and fire plugs appeared where there weren't any houses. Developments, such as Kenilworth, Beverly Hills, Grovemont, Malvern Hills, Lakeview Park, and the most elegant in Fairview called Hollywood were cut from farm land and lots advertised.

The 1903 courthouse, which had outgrown its space, was replaced with a sixteen-story granite structure on Court Plaza. Stephens-Lee High School for blacks was built on Catholic Hill within view of the city, and Douglas Ellington designed one for whites on McDowell Street.

A small burley tobacco market developed and farmers built log structures in which to cure the leaf. Money was spent for road improvement, so the farm truck could bring products and people into town. Prosperity seemed within reach as new textile and wood products industries provided plenty of non-farm jobs.

Few were prepared for the closing of the Central Bank and Trust Company on November 20, 1930. Since this bank was the main depository for county funds, the county saw its assessed valuation collapse. It shrank from almost $180,000,000 in 1927 to less than $80,000,000 in 1933. The crash took funds for school and sanitary districts, as well as money which had insured the indebtedness for both city and county.

Where the fire station is located in Skyland, C. O. Case ran a mercantile store in the 1920s. His brother Arthur was postmaster. The first Case in the area, John F., owned much land which he received as a grant from North Carolina, but life was not easy for these men as they grew up. In order to attend Newton Academy they got up at 4:30 a.m., helped with the family chores, and walked from Skyland to Biltmore Avenue. Photographs courtesy of Marion Case Havener.

Boy Scouts in this fire circle can date their beginnings in the county to 1914 when Troop I was organized at the First Congregational Church on Merrimon Avenue. Dr. J. B. Thrall and Harry Dill were leaders. The first executive of Daniel Boone Council, A. W. Allen, came to Asheville after World War I and worked with Dr. Thrall and Mr. Dill. The council was organized in 1920 with four troops and sixty-four boys in Buncombe County. Within two years it included fourteen counties of Western North Carolina. The first Daniel Boone Camp, where perhaps this William Barnhill picture was made, was located in Pisgah National Forest above Bent Creek Experiment Station. In 1941 R. Lee Ellis, president of Coca-Cola in Asheville, gave seven hundred acres in Haywood County for a Scout camp, so Daniel Boone was moved. Photograph courtesy of North Carolina Collection, Pack Memorial Public Library.

Dorothy Walls Assembly for the American Methodist Episcopal Zion Church in Black Mountain was formerly a sanitarium operated by Dr. I. J. Archer for the Fellowship of the Royal League. The fraternal organization with headquarters in Chicago built the building pictured in 1920 after a former building burned. Porches were screened as all sanitariums were at the time. This sanitarium closed in 1945 and Dr. Archer moved to Cragmont Sanitarium nearby. Photograph from the North Carolina Collection, Pack Memorial Public Library.

Grovemont, in Swannanoa, was named for E. W. Grove, the innovative man who lent his creative talent to so many projects in both city and county. Grove intended for Grovemont to be a "model town" when he designed it in the early 1920s. He built Grovestone quarry nearby to feed gravel for roads and stones for a community building and walls with entrance gates. Progress on the town stopped with Mr. Grove's untimely death in 1927. More houses were built after World War II, but Grovemont never lived up to its designer's dreams. Photograph from the North Carolina Collection, Pack Memorial Public Library.

Lake Eden, near Black Mountain, was built by E. W. Grove as a girls camp, but later changed to a summer resort. In the late 1930s trustees of Black Mountain College bought the site and used it for their unique experiment in advanced education. Camp Rockmont is located at Lake Eden and each year in late May the Black Mountain Music Festival is held there. Photograph courtesy of the North Carolina Collection, Pack Memorial Public Library.

Franklin Silas Terry, vice-president of General Electric, and his wife Lillian Emerson Terry retired to Black Mountain and built In the Oaks. In 1923 the newspaper called it the second largest private house in the state after the Biltmore House. In addition to a paneled great hall, it features an indoor swimming pool, a gymnasium/ballroom, and a bowling alley. In 1954 Mrs. Terry willed the house and one hundred acres of land to the Western North Carolina Diocese of the Episcopal Church which uses it as a conference center. Photograph courtesy of Franklin T. Perley.

Grove Park School, a fashionable finishing school for young ladies, operated in the 1920s in the former home of Dr. Carl V. Reynolds on Edgemont Road. Later Misses Laura and Lillian L. Plonk ran Plonk School of Creative Arts there. In the 1940s when it was Albemarle Inn, composer Bela Bartok was a guest. While there, he completed his Third Concerto for piano, also known as the Asheville Concerto or Concerto of Birds. The Reynolds house is now a private residence. Photograph from the North Carolina Collection, Pack Memorial Public Library.

Alonzo Carlton Reynolds, better known as A. C., served fifty-three years in education as a teacher, principal, superintendent of schools, and college president. Reynolds was born in Sandy Mush and attended Brick Church School. Several college degrees enabled him to lead Rutherford College and Cullowhee Normal and Industrial School (now Western Carolina College). During his second term as superintendent of Buncombe County schools, Reynolds began the process of consolidation within the districts. In 1927 he led the movement that founded Biltmore College and served as its first president. He retired in 1942 after serving as principal of Biltmore and Oakley High Schools. A dormitory at Western Carolina University and a Buncombe County high school are named for A. C. Reynolds. Photograph courtesy of Thomas Reynolds.

This photograph of Ebenezer School on Willow Creek Road in Sandy Mush is in bad shape, but it shows well the condition of schools in the Sandy Mush district before 1924. In that year Sandy Mush voted for fifty thousand dollars in bonds for capital outlay. Pictured are, first row left to right, Hoyle Clark, Wilder Clark, Manson Giles, Bain Scott, Nevie Clark, Thelma Duckett, Margie Duckett, Bertie Scott, Edna Hall, Lizzie Hall, Annie Dee Duckett, Agnes Clark, Hilda Duckett, and the teacher, Nora Lane. Second row, Homer Clark, Hillard Clark, Gomer Giles, Troy Duckett, Carl Clark, Fulmer Duckett, Elsie Hall, Velda Giles, Helen Hall, Dorothy Scott, and Frankie Duckett. Third row, Margaret Duckett, Lassie Duckett, and Gensie Giles. Fourth row, Columbus Barrell and Zene Duckett. Photograph courtesy of Mabel Duckett.

In 1922 J. D. Murphy and Fred Sale began buying land along Beaver Creek for an exclusive housing development to be known as Lakeview Park. Centered around a lake called Beaver Lake, it followed a plan made by city planner Dr. John Nolen. From 1923 to 1926 lots sold well, but in 1931 Beaver Lake went into the hands of the mortgage company and property changed hands several times. After World War II, Beaver Lake became important again as a major Asheville housing development. Beaver Lake was created by damming Beaver Creek and flooding what had been known as Baird Bottoms. To the left is the roof of the sales office of the development, a building that later became the clubhouse for Beaver Lake Country Club. It was removed after the Asheville Country Club took over the golf course. Photograph from the North Carolina Collection, Pack Memorial Public Library.

In the Great Smokies there's a peak named for this small man from Japan, shown photographing the Biltmore House. George Masa, photographer, ran the Plateau Studio with his friend Blake Creasman, but he is known for more than that. He loved the Smokies, hiked them extensively, and photographed them in a way others couldn't. Masa died in 1933, but he will live on in the excellence of his pictures. Photograph courtesy of Jean Creasman Lance.

A Sunday drive in the mountains became more popular as roads improved in the 1920s. Off for a trip are Elsie Drake at the wheel, Mabel Dockery on the running board, and Carrie Drake on the back seat. Photograph courtesy of Carrie Drake Bolick.

The 1922 graduates from Candler Academy called themselves the rainbow class. Instead of the traditional white, some of the young ladies wore colored dresses and the men navy blue suits. Graduates were, front row, left to right, Betty Whitside in orange; Zera Hall in green; Evelyn Morgan, white; Henrietta Clark, white; Clara Penland, lavender; Clara Jaynes, pink, and Ida Sue Gaston, white. This was the last class to graduate from Candler Academy, which was located on old Highway 10. In that year the Candler School District voted for a thirty-five thousand-dollar bond levy and a new Candler High School was built. Photograph courtesy of Zera Hall Robertson.

Growth of subdivisions in both city and county in the 1920s increased the demand for water, so in 1924 Asheville Water Department built Bee Tree Lake reservoir with a capacity of 500,000,000 gallons. The city had purchased the Bee Tree watershed in 1921 and laid a sixteen-inch pipe to bring chlorinated water to a 5,000,000 gallon concrete reservoir on Beaucatcher Mountain. Bee Tree Lake was open for recreation until the 1980s. Photograph courtesy of James H. Coman.

Another change on Pack Square in 1926 was a new library building which replaced the old bank building given by George Pack in 1899. This Pack Square building of white Georgia marble served Pack Memorial Public Library until it moved to Haywood street in 1979. It is now included in Pack Place Education Arts and Science Center to house the Asheville Art Museum. Photograph from the North Carolina Collection, Pack Memorial Public Library.

Courthouse offices that are spilling into annex buildings today had a precedent set for them when the 1903 courthouse proved to be inadequate and other offices had to be found. In his book Historical Facts Concerning Buncombe County Government, County Registrar George Diggs described conditions that existed in 1922 when the commissioners began to talk of the need for a new courthouse. This has been slightly edited. "In the old Court House records pertaining to the Clerk's office were scattered from the basement to the attic; records of the Tax Collector's office piled on top of each other for lack of space; records in the Register of Deeds' office were without fire protection, and the county treasurer had to transact business within the confines of a small office. The Sheriff's Department had three small rooms and the Solicitor one. There were two terms of court every month and only one court chamber. The County Engineer and Draftsman were located over the county garage, the Board of Education in the new court house (meaning an annex), the Juvenile Court in the Law Building, Health Department in another building, the County Commissioners in three small rooms in the Reynolds building, and the County Auditor in the same building with his records piled three and four deep." The house owned by Mrs. M. H. Harris, which faced College Street, was one of the annexes. The county commissioners bought this property in February 1924 from Mrs. Harris for $215,000. The land was to be used for a new courthouse. Photograph from the book by Mr. Diggs.

123

When new courthouse and city hall buildings were being considered, Art Deco architect Douglas Ellington submitted a sketch of matching buildings. At a meeting July 6, 1926, city and county officials agreed to build matching buildings on a site owned by the county just east of the 1903 courthouse. Land between the new buildings and Spruce Street was to be a public park. Buncombe County minutes of November 10, 1926, include a letter from the commissioners to the mayor and city commissioners expressing displeasure because Ellington had submitted a design for the park without consulting both governmental bodies. This must have developed into more of a problem because later the commissioners wrote to the Asheville Chamber of Commerce protesting the hiring of Douglas Ellington as architect of the buildings without consulting county officials. Pictured is Ellington's sketch of the matching buildings which he hoped to see built. The structure joining the city and county buildings would have housed a bus station. Asheville City officials used the Ellington design. County officials did not. Photograph courtesy of Historic Resources Commission.

One of the last photographs of the Buncombe County courthouse built in 1903 facing College Street shows its proximity to the new courthouse opened in 1928. The 1903 court house was built on land deeded by George Pack. Shortly after the 1903 courthouse was built, the 1876 courthouse was taken down from Public Square. The square was deeded to the City of Asheville and renamed for Mr. Pack. Photograph courtesy of the North Carolina Collection, Pack Memorial Public Library.

The village of Fairview in 1925 boasted at least three stores, a phone company, a gristmill, a blacksmith shop, and a post office. Boss Earley ran the garage. Photograph courtesy of Mr. and Mrs. Everett Ledbetter.

Facing page bottom left: The Asheville City Hall, designed by Art Deco artist Douglas Ellington, was dedicated March 19, 1928. Built of brick and pink marble, the City Hall is topped by a pink and green tile roof. Its classical design and unusual decorative features make it outstanding among Art Deco buildings in the United States. Photograph courtesy of James H. Coman.

The Buncombe County Courthouse, designed by Milburn and Heister of Washington, D. C., was dedicated December 1, 1928. The building, built of brick and Tennessee limestone, features granite columns at the entrance. These are repeated at the top to ornament the jail section. Photograph courtesy of James H. Coman.

Biltmore High School on Biltmore Avenue was built in 1926-1927 after the Biltmore District voted for $250,000 in bonds for capital outlay. At that time bonds were issued by district. The building also housed Buncombe Junior College, the first tuition-free junior college in North Carolina. Asheville opened the College of the City of Asheville in 1928. During the Depression the colleges were combined under the name Asheville-Biltmore and continued to meet at Biltmore High School. The college moved into David Millard Junior High School in 1934, to Asheville Normal School, to the former Children's Home Building on Merrimon Avenue, and into Seeley's Castle in 1949. In 1961 it moved to the present campus off Weaver Boulevard. Elementary students occupied the Biltmore building after the high school students moved to T. C. Roberson in 1962. Recently, Biltmore School has been used for offices for the Buncombe County Schools. In 1992 the Buncombe County Sheriff's Department is scheduled to occupy the building. Photograph from the North Carolina Collection, Pack Memorial Public Library.

To a coon hunter there is nothing like the sound of a good coon dog at night. Back after a successful 1927 hunt are four hunters and their kill for the night. They are, left to right, Hubert Capps, Marlow F. Pullian, Dr. J. E. Owen, and Zed Henderson. The house in the background is on Flint Street, the home of a Mrs. Sanders. Photograph courtesy of Ramona Henderson Bryson.

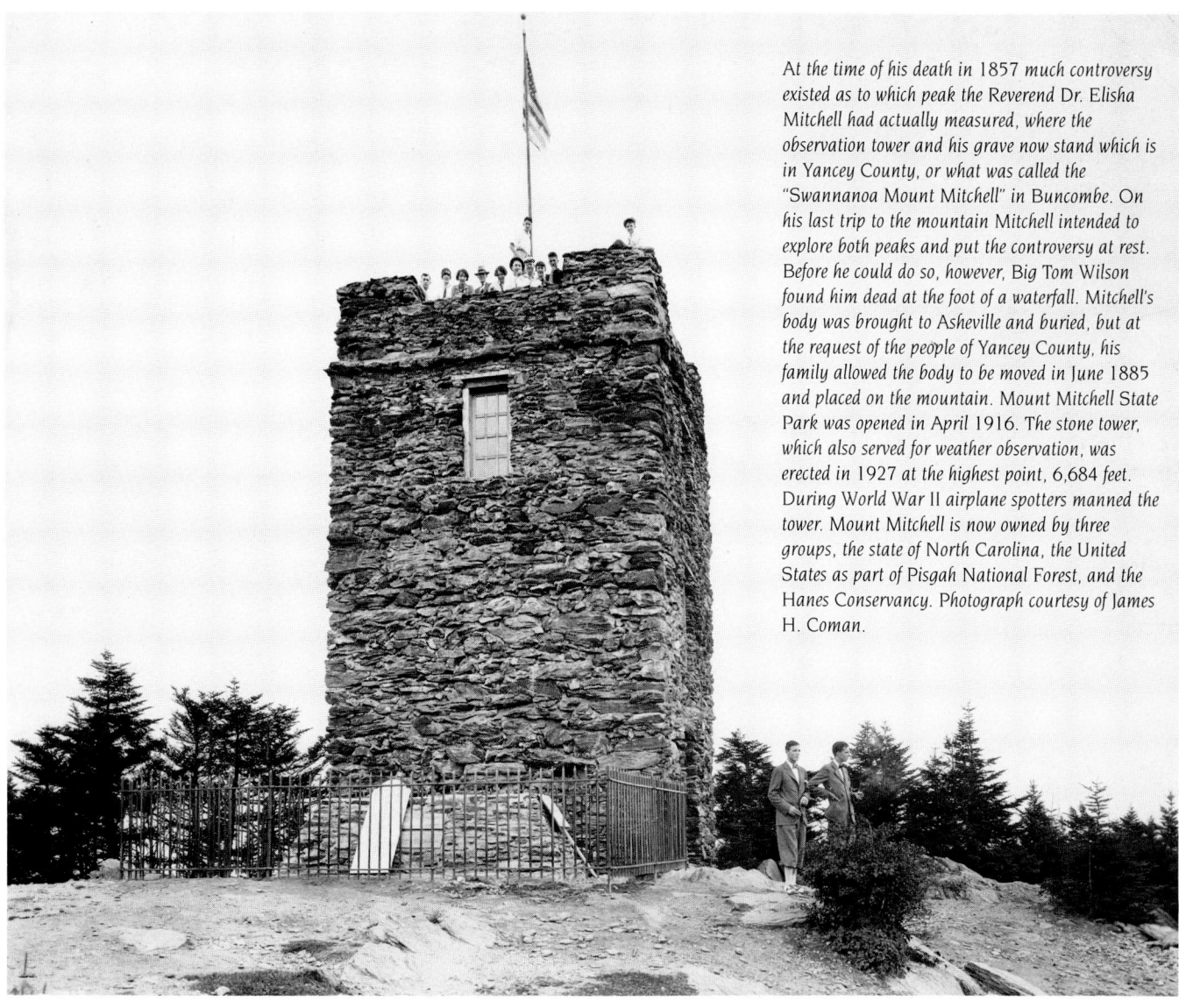

At the time of his death in 1857 much controversy existed as to which peak the Reverend Dr. Elisha Mitchell had actually measured, where the observation tower and his grave now stand which is in Yancey County, or what was called the "Swannanoa Mount Mitchell" in Buncombe. On his last trip to the mountain Mitchell intended to explore both peaks and put the controversy at rest. Before he could do so, however, Big Tom Wilson found him dead at the foot of a waterfall. Mitchell's body was brought to Asheville and buried, but at the request of the people of Yancey County, his family allowed the body to be moved in June 1885 and placed on the mountain. Mount Mitchell State Park was opened in April 1916. The stone tower, which also served for weather observation, was erected in 1927 at the highest point, 6,684 feet. During World War II airplane spotters manned the tower. Mount Mitchell is now owned by three groups, the state of North Carolina, the United States as part of Pisgah National Forest, and the Hanes Conservancy. Photograph courtesy of James H. Coman.

Anyone who rode a train in the days of steam will remember handcars with maintenance crews used to move up and down the rails. Two men pumped see-saw fashion on the handle in the middle to make the car go. This crew was often seen working on the Southern Railway around 1915. Seated are John Burgin and Perk Daugherty. Standing are the foreman R. L. Bugg, James (Potts) Lytle, Harry Davidson, Iddie Daugherty, Garfield Daugherty, and Walter Dillingham. Photograph courtesy of the Valley Museum, Black Mountain.

Liberty school, at the corner of Monte Vista Road and Pete Luther Road, was one of Buncombe County's two-room schools. Children in the "big room," grades 4-7, in 1928 were taught by Miss Terrie Petit. Since the school was heated with a coal stove, boys took turns carrying coal and water. Students brought their lunch in a bucket and each one had a folding metal cup. Restrooms were outhouses behind the school. In the "big room" were, front row, left to right, Lowell Robinson, Martin McElreath, Willie Jamison, Porter Daniels, John Chockley, Walter Chockley, Everett Lance, and Clarence Earley. Middle row, Juanita Earley, Macy Lance, Deana Rhymer, Florence Jamison, Mabel Baker, Louise Chockley, Mary Lee Robinson, Doris Lance, Fannie Green, and Margaret Pressley. Top row, Bryan Green, Milburn Parham, Carl Pressley, Miss Petit, Clyde Robinson, A. P. Thrash, Howard Penley, and Willia Cathey. Photograph courtesy of Doris Lance Plemmons.

127

LANGREN
RAYS STUDIO
PORTRAITS COMMERCIAL AND KODAK WORK
ROBERT LEE SMITH & CO.
REALTORS
PACK SQUARE CANDY KITCHEN
CHOP SUEY
PETRIE
C.D. KENNY CO.
DRUGS
113
SAFETY CAR
FRONT ENTRANCE
107
SAFETY CAR

Time to Tighten the Belt

1930 to 1940

10

Bondholders united and began negotiations concerning money owed to them after the collapse of Central Bank and Trust Company. Settlement was time-consuming but in the end the community was rescued from bankruptcy. A system of paying back what was owed was established.

Agencies, such as the Civilian Conservation Corp and the Works Progress Administration, and loans from the federal government relieved a lot of the economic readjustments the county had to make because of the Depression. The Forest Service and the Rural Electrification Administration helped, also.

Life may have been easier for the farmer than the city dweller during the Depression. He still lived without electricity. Wells and springs provided his water. If he had no gas to run trucks and tractors, he had his mules and horses.

When people say, "Asheville isn't what it used to be," they mean the trolley system, controlled at Pack Square, is gone. Asheville had the second electric streetcar system in the nation. Cars could bring people to town from Weaverville, West Asheville, North Asheville, Sunset Mountain, Biltmore, and Montford. Photograph from the Ball Collection, Southern Research Library, University of North Carolina.

129

With the help of the Rosewald Foundation, black children in Swannanoa and Black Mountain were able to go to school near their homes. Shown with the students about 1930 is the teacher James T. Sapp. Photograph courtesy of the Valley Museum, Black Mountain.

To provide wood during the Depression, the Forest Service set up the Asheville Community Wood Yard beside the French Broad on the West Asheville side of the Haywood Street Bridge. Men out of work cut roads into the Bent Creek Research and Demonstration Forest and hauled out dead trees to give away. Photographs courtesy of Bent Creek Research and Demonstration Forest.

Margaret Abell, one of the first women to work for the Forest Service, was a researcher at the experiment station at Bent Creek during the 1930s. The U.S. Department of Agriculture established the Appalachian Forest Experiment Station in Buncombe County in 1921 and Bent Creek became the station's first experimental forest. Early work included dividing its cutover stands like the one pictured into fifty-acre research areas with boundary markers and plans for studying each. Today Bent Creek has 6,300 acres of experimental forest. Photograph courtesy of Bent Creek Research and Demonstration Forest.

Work provided by the government during the Depression helped the county weather its hard times. In Black Mountain the Works Progress Administration built the dam at Lake Tomahawk. The lake was designed to develop the town's tourist potential, but it is seeing more use today than ever before. Photograph courtesy of James H. Coman.

On Septembr 4, 1934, Asheville streetcars took their last ride. People lined up at Pritchard Park for one last look as the electric trolley was replaced with a bus system. As streets were repaved, tracks were covered. Some were removed in World War II to be sold for scrap metal. However, as long as one person remains who rode the cars, Asheville will have a love affair with the electric trolley. Photograph courtesy of the North Carolina Collection, Pack Memorial Public Library.

Doors at the Beech Presbyterian Church were constructed from a massive yellow poplar tree that was a landmark in the Beech community. The tree was 150 feet tall, 39 feet around, and estimated to be 350 years old. It was so large it had holes in it where boys could hide. When it burned on April 14, 1935, the community thought a fire might have been started in one of those holes. This photograph of the tree is by William Barnhill. The man is unidentified. Photograph courtesy of the North Carolina Collection, Pack Memorial Public Library.

Each child in "Pat" Rhea's Sunday School class at Beech Presbyterian Church raised one chicken as a contribution to the Lords Acre Project. On this Sunday, circa 1936, the children brought their chickens to church. The Lord's Acre Project, directed by the Reverend Dumont Clarke, grew to be international in scope. It served a need for people to give at a time when they had no money. One women saved her Sunday eggs. Another set aside one hen, and all the eggs that hen laid went to the Lord. Photograph courtesy of "Pat" Rhea Hensley.

In 1937 the state opened the Western North Carolina Sanitarium to care for tubercular patients. It offered care for fifty cents to a dollar fifty a day, including medical fees The sanitarium was the last tuberculosis hospital to operate in the county. In 1979 it became a drug detoxification unit and a home for the mentally retarded. Photograph from the North Carolina Collection, Pack Memorial Public Library.

Thomas Wolfe spent the summer of 1937 living and writing in a cabin, on or near the Asheville Recreation Park, that belonged to his friend Max Whitson. He was a tireless worker, according to accounts of those who knew him, smoked a lot, and drank a lot. Though his first novel Look Homeward Angel was scorned by the press and others in Asheville, he was sought after while he was here. Former friends came to call and crowds followed him around the streets of town. That was Wolfe's last trip home. He died in Baltimore a year later of tuberculosis of the brain. Photograph courtesy of James H. Coman.

Author Thomas Wolfe's death at thirty-eight shocked those who had begun to appreciate his genius. Funeral services were held at the First Presbyterian Church in Asheville and burial was at Riverside Cemetery. Riverside was established in 1885 by the Asheville Cemetery Company, Incorporated. Graves from older cemeteries were moved to Riverside, so it contains the remains of many of the county's founders. Graves to be found there with Wolfe include Zebulon B. Vance, Richmond Pearson, and William Sidney Porter (O'Henry). Photograph courtesy of James H. Coman.

Young men from the Farm School at Swannanoa, now Warren Wilson College, earned scholarship money laying the foundation for Beech Presbyterian Church. It is estimated that over ten-thousand volunteer hours went into the building of the church. Photograph courtesy of "Pat" Rhea Hensley.

In the 1930s and 40s a Farmer's Federation program directed by the Reverend Dumont Clarke encouraged church people to grow an acre of food for the Lord for every ten for themselves. These young people at Beech are hoeing potatoes which they will sell to support the building of the Beech Presbyterian Church. With them in the field is the Reverend W. M. Hyde, pastor at Beech for more than thirty years. In the background is the Beech school for grades one through nine. This building is now used for activities of the Beech Community Club. Photograph courtesy of "Pat" Rhea Hensley.

Civilian Conservation Corp workers housed at the Bent Creek Experimental Forest Station in the 1930s built a number of structures that remain in use. This house supported by rough-hewn timbers served as bunk house and mess hall for researchers. It is now the office of the Project Leader. Photograph courtesy of Bent Creek Research and Demonstration Forest.

"I baptize thee in the name of the Father, the Son, and the Holy Ghost." The Reverend Erskine Plemmons, pastor of Mt. Carmel Baptist Church, baptized his converts in 1939 in a spring-fed farm pond at Ed Sluder's on the Old Leicester Highway. Photograph courtesy of the Reverend Mr. Plemmons.

Buncombe County historian Dr. Foster A. Sondley was born in Alexander and lived all his life in the county. He owned an extensive library of historical materials which he left to Pack Memorial Library when he died in 1931. Sondley published several histories, but the one he is best known for is the two-volume set published in 1930. Photograph from the North Carolina Collection, Pack Memorial Public Library.

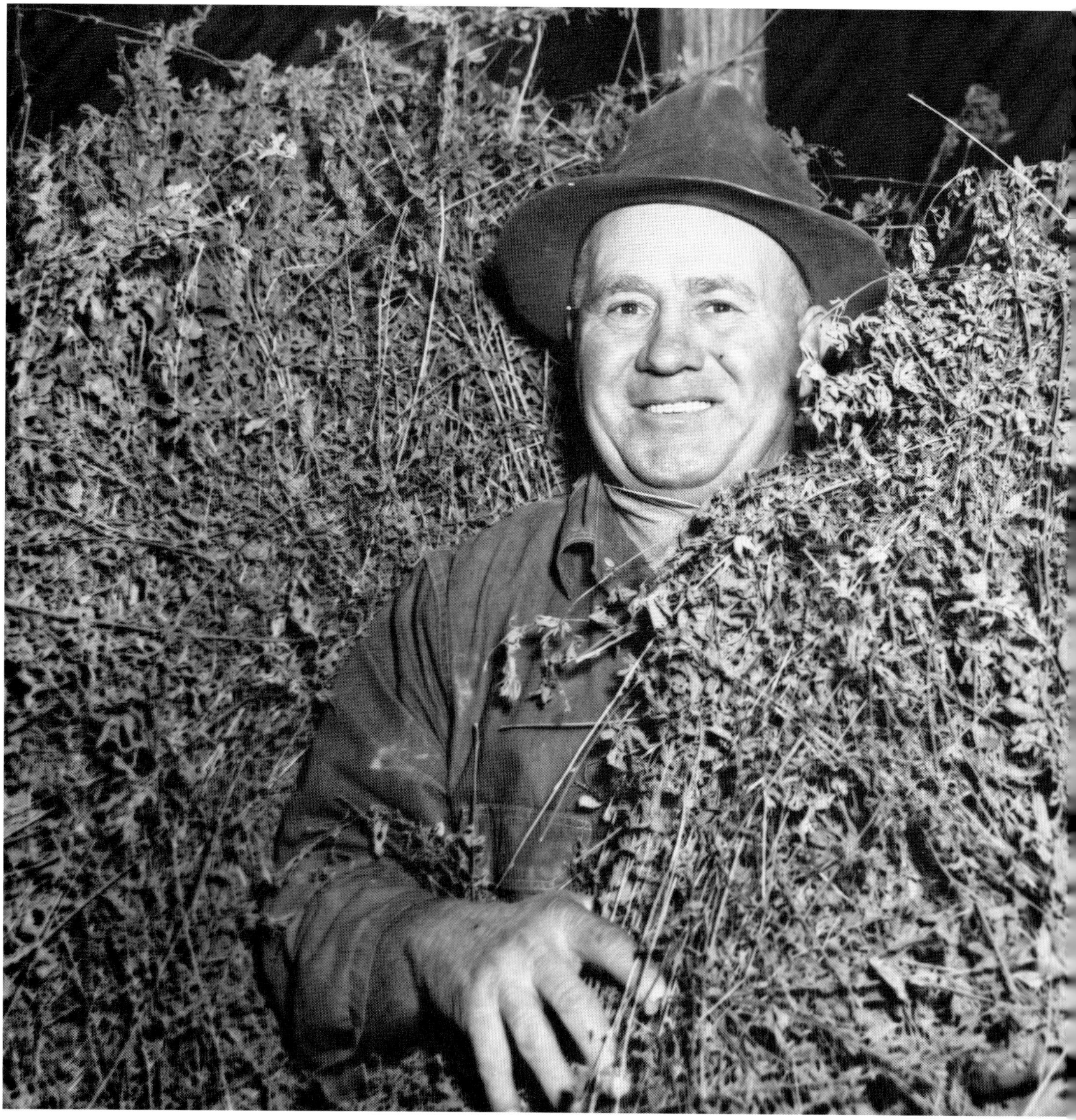

War and Its Aftermath

1940 to 1960

11

All else paled into insignificance during World War II. Asheville rented the City Building to the Air Weather Wing and moved its offices into the county courthouse. Postal Accounts took over the Grove Arcade.

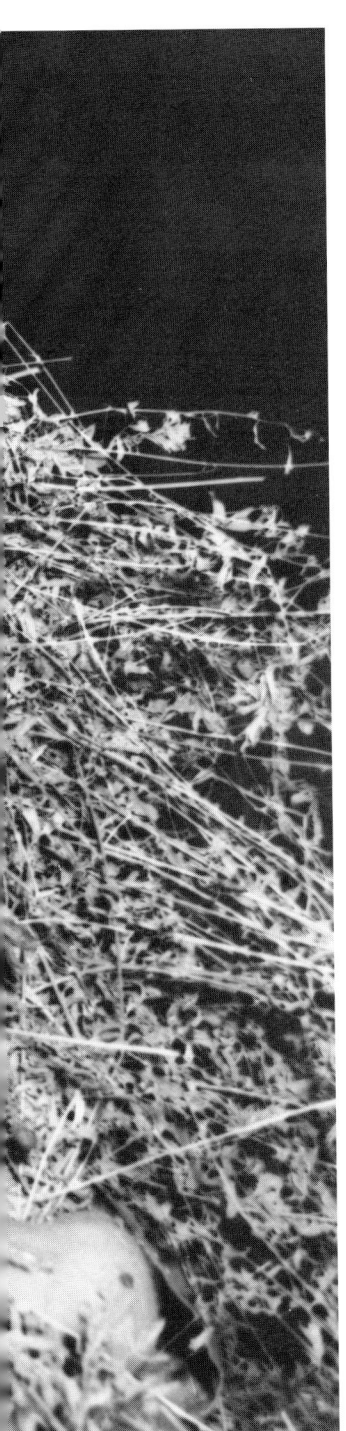

The beauty of the mountains made the county a favorite spot for servicemen on leave. Returning wounded crowded hospital facilities, such as Oteen Hospital and Moore General at Swannanoa. The Army rented Sand Hill High School, which was still unfinished, and used it for a hospital.

Economically the county was still depressed. Schools and roads were needed but because of the large indebtedness and low income, a limit was placed on the amount that could be raised by the sale of bonds. A school committee of prominent citizens drew up a wish list and for the first time in Buncombe's history a county-wide vote passed a bond issue for schools.

Men returning from the war found few jobs, though the industrial base had begun to grow. An exodus of manpower took young men to the north. The growth of county population slowed from 1950 to 1960.

One of the first farmers to grow alfalfa in Buncombe County was Milton Roberson of Candler, shown here in 1945 with part of his crop. Roberson worked throughout his life in organizations that benefited the farmer. One of the first committeemen of the Agriculture Stabilization and Conservation Service, he also worked with the Grange, the Farm Extension office, and other programs. Photograph from The Farmer's Federation News.

Almost every event during World War II set up booths to sell United States War Bonds. This man brought thirty dollars in pennies and nickels to buy a bond for his baby, plus some additional stamps at the Farmer's Federation picnic in Asheville, July 15, 1943. Virginia Osborne and Maxine Ingle of West Buncombe were selling the bonds. Photograph courtesy of James McClure Clarke.

Dancing teacher Beale Fletcher taught daughter Maria balance at an early age. When she was grown, Maria Beale Fletcher danced her way to fame as Miss America 1962. Photograph courtesy of Bertha Fletcher Holland.

With twenty-five hundred dollars from the Presbyterian Church USA and ten thousand volunteer hours, members of the Beech Presbyterian Church were able to worship in a new stone building in 1941. Present at this late winter dedication service were the building supervisor Jake Penland, the Reverend D. Cleland McAfee, former secretary of foreign missions, and the Reverend W. M. Hyde, who served the church as pastor for about thirty years. Photograph courtesy of "Pat" Rhea Hensley.

Ensign Elspeth McClure, United States Naval Womens Reserve, and Lt. James McClure Clarke, United States Naval Reserve, were married February 17, 1945, at the First Presbyterian Church in Asheville. Ensign McClure, daughter of James G. K. McClure, was stationed in Charleston. Lieutenant Clarke, son of Dr. and Mrs. Dumont Clarke was stationed in Washington after 19 months service in the Pacific. Following the war the Clarkes lived in Hickory Nut Gap. Mr. Clarke was representative to Congress, 1982 to 1984, and 1986 to 1990. Photograph courtesy of James McClure Clarke.

The end of WWII brought men back to the farms, to school, and to their jobs. In Western North Carolina jobs were scarce, forcing veterans to move from Buncombe and look for employment in the north where there was work. This touching picture, made in Haywood County, shows Seaman First Class John Singleton being greeted by his aunt Mrs. Frank Guy. Photograph courtesy of James McClure Clarke.

On Easter morning, April 6, 1947, William Vance and Betty Osborne Henry drove their family to Acton United Methodist Church in a pony cart. With Bill and Betty are Beth and Jimmie Henry. The pony is Dixie. Photograph courtesy of William Vance Henry.

Theron Tweed was about three when he rode a load of tobacco sticks behind his father's workhorse. In the background is a typical Buncombe county farm. Tobacco allotments are determined by the Agriculture Stabilization an Conservation Service. The rest of land may grow corn, hay, or be turned over to pasture. Photograph courtesy of Mabel Duckett.

Most of these "old timers" at the 1948 Fourth of July picnic at Beech would tell you they had attended every picnic since they were children. Chloris Penland Rhea, on the left, was ten years old in 1884 when the event was begun by the Reverend A. M. Penland as an end-of-school exercise. "Old-timers" seated left to right, Mrs. Rhea, Martha Buckner, Mrs. Henry Henderson, Mrs. David Scott. Standing, George Donkel, Henry Henderson, Henry Farmer, J. E. Carter, Vasco Ballard, D. M. Donkel, and F. A. Penland. Photograph courtesy of "Pat" Rhea Hensley.

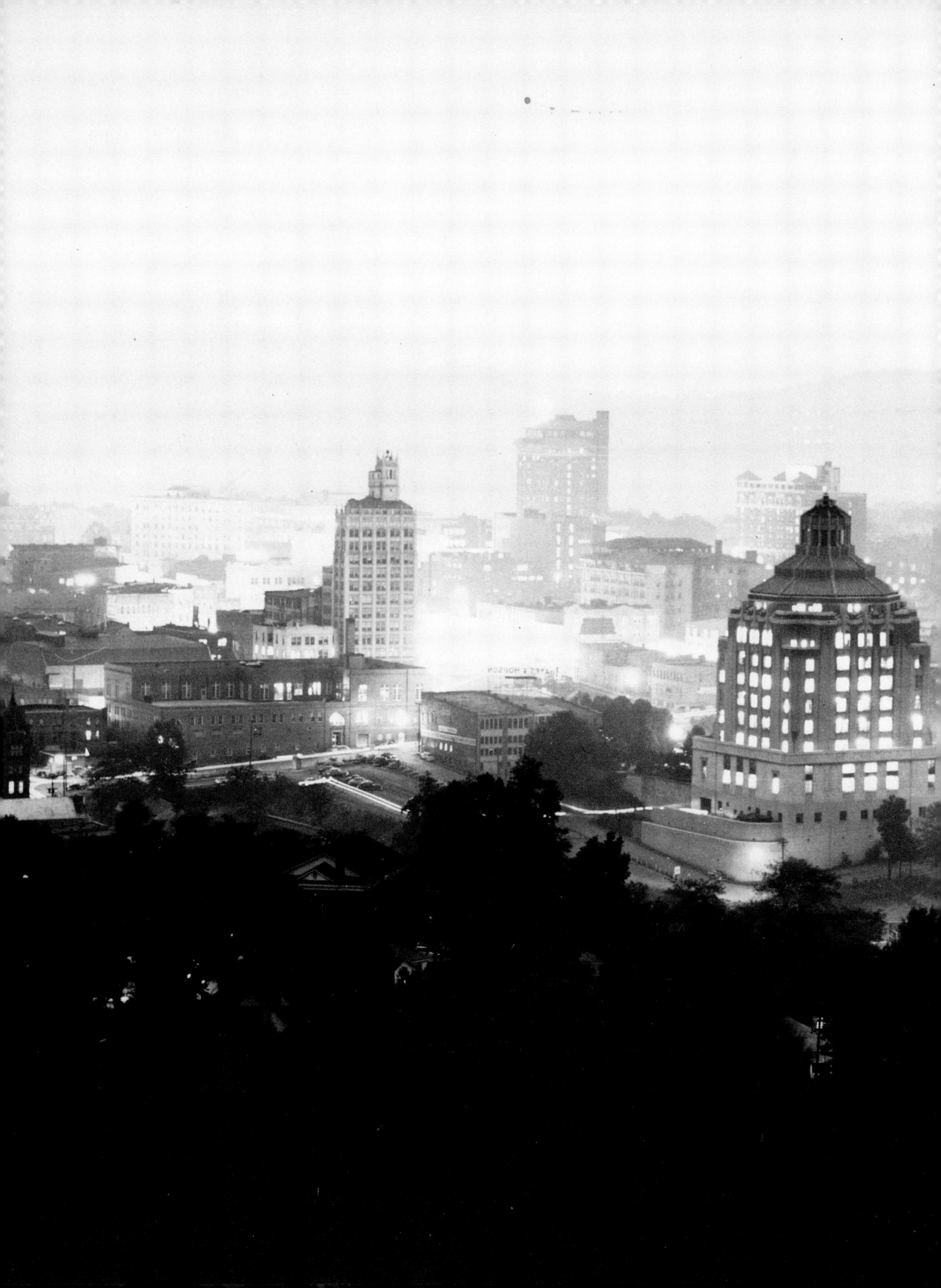

Rain and fog diffuse the lights of downtown Asheville in this memorable view taken from Beaucatcher Mountain. In the City Hall all lights are aglow, a contrast to the County Court House, where all is quiet except the jail in the upper stories. Longtime residents will recognize the Langren Hotel as part of the skyline. The Biltmore Building and BB&T are not. Photograph courtesy of James H. Coman.

Memorial Mission Hospital came into being when four local hospitals combined. They were Mission Hospital, formerly located on Woodfin Street at Charlotte; Biltmore Hospital, formerly Clarence Barker Memorial, in Biltmore Village; the Asheville Colored Hospital at Biltmore Avenue and Southwide, and Victoria Hospital, formerly Norburn Hospital. The contract was finalized in 1950 when Victoria donated the land and Florence Stephenson Hall to Mission. Almost immediately land was broken for a five-story wing to the north, shown here. Florence Stephenson Hall continued to serve until 1982 when another building project began. Today Mission has a wide reputation as a regional health facility. Photograph courtesy of James H. Coman.

Dr. Allen Brewton, company doctor for American Enka, kept watch on Robert Mitchum on the set of Thunder Road. The movie about running bootlegged whiskey in the hills was shot at several locations in the county. Photograph courtesy of Sara Roberson Long.

T. C. Roberson took the job of Superintendent of Buncombe County Schools on January 1, 1935, and served for thirty-four years. At ceremonies held for his retirement, his accomplishments were summarized by Congressman Roy A. Taylor, "During the 34-year period, 21 high schools consolidated into six modern facilities . . . 45 elementary schools, 14 of them one-room, consolidated into 27 modern plants, all accredited . . . average number of pupils per teacher reduced from 37 to 27 and the annual number of high school graduates increased from 475 to 1,269." T. C. Roberson's slogan was "The Child First." Photograph courtesy of Mrs. T. C. Roberson.

The Citizens Committee for Better Schools, the Buncombe County School Board, and the Asheville City School Board received national recognition for the consolidation of twenty-six school tax districts to pass a $5,500,000 bond issue for school construction in 1950. As the Minneapolis Sunday Tribune pointed out, "Buncombe County, North Carolina, and its largest city, Asheville, had at least one thing in common. The school buildings were falling apart." Look Magazine in the issue of March 13, 1951, devoted several pages to the story. As a result, the "All American Certificate" was presented to Asheville and Buncombe County by Roy E. Larsen of New York, President of Time Incorporated and Chairman of the National Citizens' Committee for Public Schools, on behalf of the National Municipal League. Ceremonies were held in the Asheville City Auditorium on April 3, 1952. Photograph courtesy of Mrs. T. C. Roberson.

Various locations have served as markets for truck farmers through the years. Lexington Avenue, known as Water Street in the beginning because of fresh-water springs where farmers could water their horses, became a street of livery stables, farm supply stores, and produce markets. The double doors on many of the buildings on the street are there because farmers could back their wagons or trucks inside to unload. For many years farmers operated an outdoor produce market in the parking lot on Lexington that borders I-240. Photograph courtesy of James H. Coman.

As industry began moving into Buncombe County in the late 1950s, it became important to provide industrial training for the many workers who would be needed. As a result Asheville Buncombe Technical Institute was born in 1959. From its beginning in these buildings the school has grown to community college status with a student body of thirty thousand. The emphasis is still on vocational studies, but students may gain an associate of science or associate of arts degree which will transfer to any other college or university. Photograph courtesy of James H. Coman.

Growing tobacco is a year-round job. By the time the crop is sold in the fall, it's time to sterilize another seed bed and start again. In the summer, if the farmer has escaped leaf mold and the tobacco has grown as tall as a man, the work of "suckering" begins. Suckers grow under the leaves close to the stem. They and the flower must be pulled off or the tobacco will go to seed. Photograph courtesy James H. Coman.

Tobacco is cut in late summer and hung on sticks to dry in the field. This is when the farmer prays that it won't rain until he gets it in the barn. Picture courtesy of James H. Coman.

In a few weeks tobacco leaves are hauled to the barn and hung on tiers. For proper drying it's important for the air to circulate among the leaves. The tobacco hangs until cold weather arrives in the hills. Picture by Bob Lindsey, courtesy of James H. Coman.

In the past it took a good winter rain or snow for the tobacco to "come in case" before it could be prepared for market. Usually about November the leaves were dry enough, but moisture was needed before the farmer could work them. The whole family helped tie bundles of the leaves together. Schools in the county excused students so they could help. On today's market leaves are no longer tied. Photograph courtesy of James McClure Clark.

Until recently, tied tobacco was piled in a wide basket and hauled to market in the family truck. Grades of tobacco were marked with paper to separate them. Clyde Duckett is shown on his truck in 1947 before he took it to a large warehouse in Asheville. Photograph courtesy of Mabel Duckett.

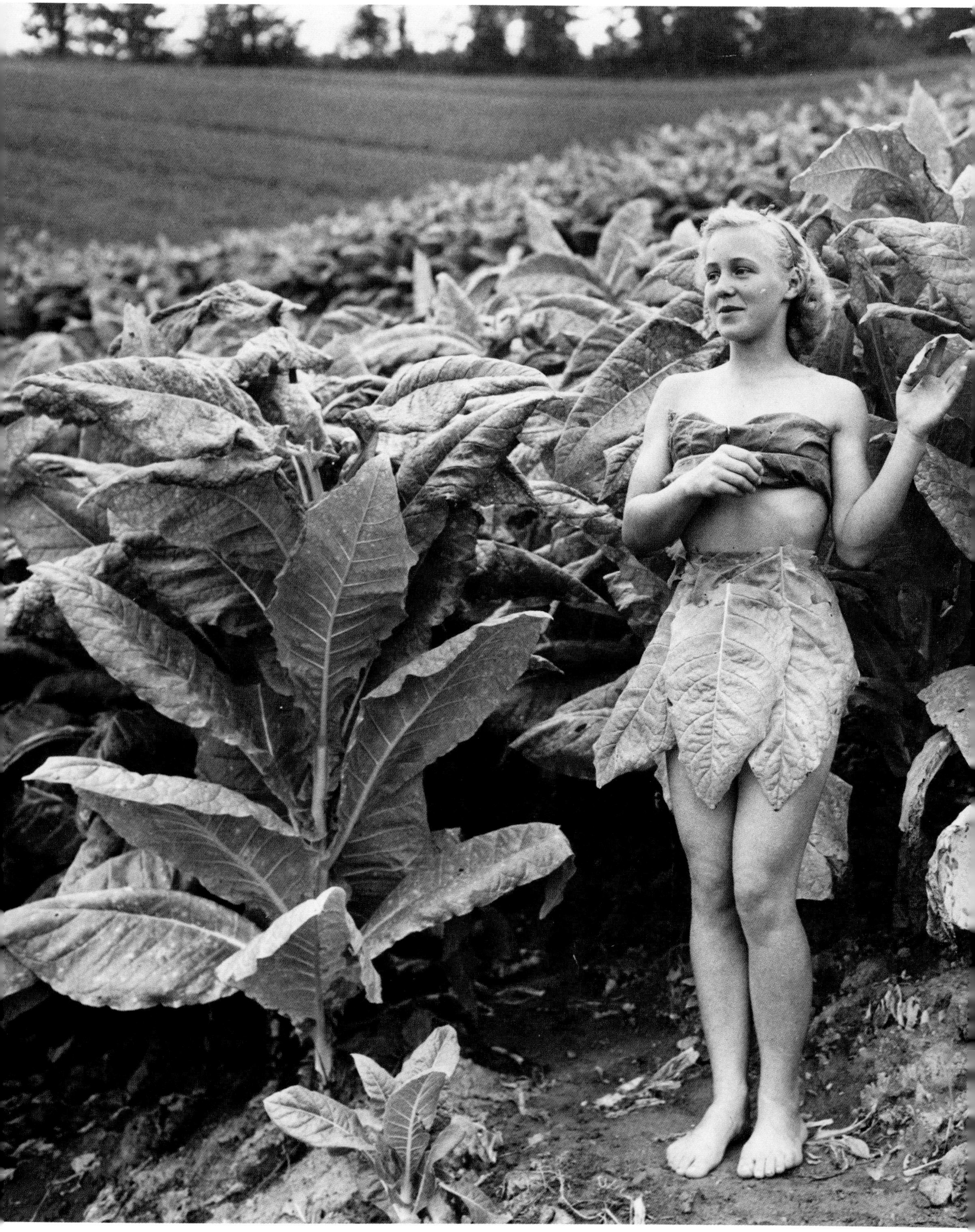

When the baskets hit the auction floor, the talk and buying are rapid. In a single day a good auctioneer can clear a warehouse. Photograph courtesy of James H. Coman.

Farmer's Federation Tobacco Queen for 1946 was Lena Zimmerman of Buncombe County, shown doing the hula in a field of burley tobacco. Actually, the queen had other duties serving as ambassador for the growing tobacco industry. Miss Zimmerman was chosen by the Asheville Junior Chamber of Commerce. Photograph from the Farmers Federation News.

No matter what year it is, the sweetest memories for children are of vacations from school, long, lazy days, and ice cream cones. Nancy Rice and Christine Cogburn share a secret as they enjoy their ice cream. Photograph courtesy of Eleanor N. Rice.

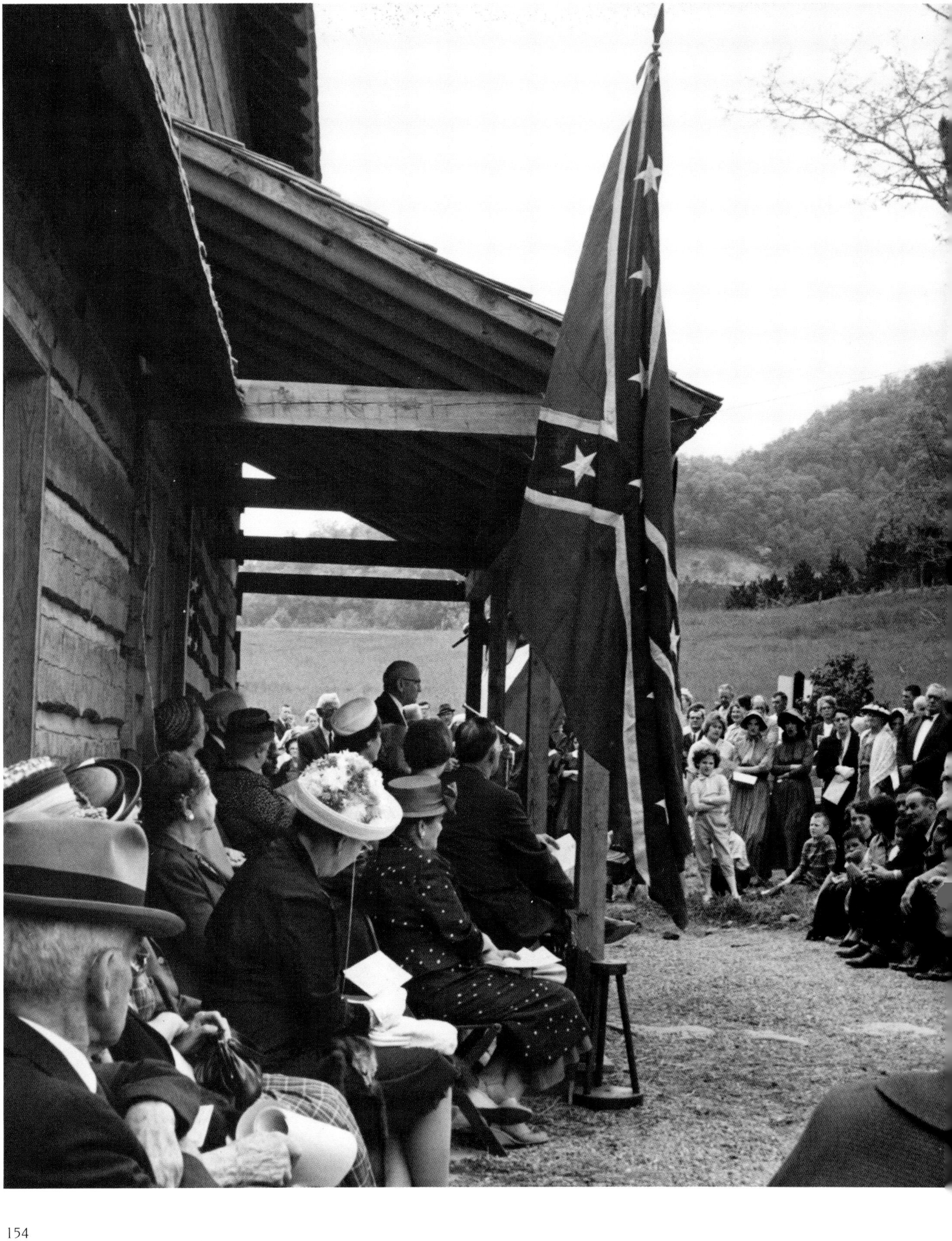

Jobs and Roads
1960 to 1980

12

Federal money flowed out of Washington and Buncombe County garnered a share. First came roads, I-40 and I-26. Then Appalachian Funds supplied the 19/23 corridor to Madison County. Social programs like Model Cities and the Opportunity Corporation gave poor people a chance to express their needs.

Housing built for the poor in the city and county filled up. Urban redevelopment changed the face of East Riverside and added new buildings to streets downtown. The city annexed more territory, added liquor by the drink, and built more shopping malls.

A growing diversified industrial development required a larger number of skilled workers. To supply these men and women, Asheville-Buncombe Technical Institute was born and six new county high schools and Asheville High School gained vocational departments.

Black children entered Asheville schools in 1961 and the county accepted twelve black children into Haw Creek School in August, 1963. The School Board set up a plan for integration of all county schools by 1966.

Tobacco was still the "money crop" but the Agricultural Experiment Stations and County Extension Agents were trying to diversify the family farm. Rural people still resisted school consolidation, and Sandy Mush refused workers from the Opportunity Corporation.

Dedication of the Vance home as a memorial to former Governor and U.S. Sen. Zebulon Baird Vance was held on May 13, 1961, 130 years after the colorful statesman saw the light of day in the home of his grandfather, Col. David Vance. Recreating the Vance homestead had been discussed by many for more than half a century, but it took the effort of the North Carolina Department of Archives and History, a commission headed by D. Hiden Ramsey, and many citizens of the county to make it happen. While foreman Gregg Sawyer and carpenters George Whitaker and Paul Whittemore carefully replaced the red clay between the handmade bricks with cement, Robert Conway, historic sites specialist, looked for materials. Logs in the two story section of the house had to be 28 feet long, so Conway used new ones cut from land owned by the American Enka Corporation. The spring house and loom house were built of old logs purchased from Leonard Rhea. The slaves house had belonged to Robert Patton of Swannanoa. Rails for fences came from Macon and Yancey Counties, the corn crib from Yancey, and the smoke house from the Johanna Fox property in the Jupiter section of Buncombe County. Paneling in the sitting room, flooring in the kitchen, and the old hearth are from the old house. Both buildings and furnishings are authentic to the life of a well-to-do pioneer in the 1780s. William W. Dodge, Jr., architect, emphasized that. The memorial, located on Reems Creek Road, is open each day as a State Historic Site. Photograph courtesy of James H. Coman.

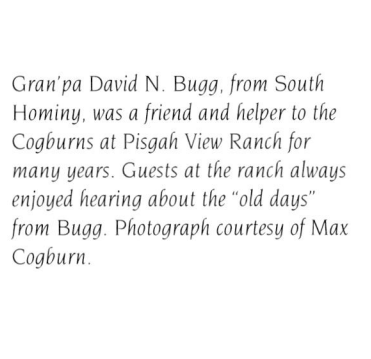

Gran'pa David N. Bugg, from South Hominy, was a friend and helper to the Cogburns at Pisgah View Ranch for many years. Guests at the ranch always enjoyed hearing about the "old days" from Bugg. Photograph courtesy of Max Cogburn.

Girl Scout Troop No. 29 of Enka-Candler won their badge in roller skating in 1961 after several sessions at the Enka Rollerama. Leaders of the troop were Sara Long and Bernice Clark. Skaters are, front row, left to right, Sharon Harris, Sharon Peebles, Linda Young, Kay McCall, Kirby Burton, Jo Anne Cole, Kathryn Long, Mary Long, and Susan Hamilton. Back row, Sally Hall Clark, Jean Brown, Glenda Leatherwood, Judy Miller, Dara Llewellyn, Jean Watkins, Kathy DeBord, and Linda Rhodes. Photograph courtesy of Sara Roberson Long.

In 1960 Owen airfield and race track were located on Amboy Road where the New Asheville Speedway is now. First developer of this land was Edwin George Carrier, who ran a streetcar along what is now Amboy and developed an amusement park in this area. Bell Sand Company is in the foreground. Photograph courtesy of Historic Resources Commission.

What to do with garbage has always been a problem for the county. In the 1960s the riverbank became the dump. Sites in what is now the town of Woodfin have also been used, one near the Burlington Plant. The present site, now almost filled, is downriver from there. Riverside Cemetery shows on the hill to the right of Riverside Drive. Just below it is an old incinerator. Most of the riverbank that is covered with litter in this picture is now home to junkyards. Photograph courtesy of Historic Resources Commission.

Money for urban renewal reached Buncombe County in the late 1960s and a massive project began off the Crosstown Expressway, now I-240. In this photograph new buildings for the Sheraton Hotel, the Young Men's Christian Association, and the Buncombe County Health and Welfare Departments have been built. The old Woodfin House is still standing where the Clyde Savings and Loan Company would be later, and a vacant lot is across from the Thomas Wolfe House where the Radisson Hotel would be built. Photograph courtesy of James H. Coman.

Pack Memorial Public Library corner with it kiosk and book depository has become a popular meeting spot in downtown Asheville since the library moved to Haywood Street in the 1960s. Photograph courtesy of James H. Coman.

Labor Day parades were popular in the county for many years. This picture of a parade float shows the street framework of the Northwestern Bank Building, now the BB&T building, on the west side of Pack Square. The bank building was completed in 1964. Photograph courtesy of Ramona Henderson Bryson.

For years audiences at the Mountain Dance and Folk Festival enjoyed the antics of "Red" Parham. A cross between a comedian and a musician, Parham could bring down the house with the animal sounds that came from his harmonica. Brother "Chubb" accompanied him on the guitar. Mountain Dance and Folk Festival was given birth by Bascombe Lamar Lunsford in 1927. It has been continued by the Asheville Area Chamber of Commerce. Photograph by Bob Lindsey, courtesy of David Holt.

Vacation Bible School is a June ritual for county and city children. Most of them, even when they're grown, can bring out pictures and tell of the fun they had. This crowd, circa 1968, is filling the steps of Oakley Baptist Church. Photograph by Juanita Wilson, courtesy of Cecelia Rhodes.

When Federal money became available for parks in the late 1970s, Asheville Recreation Park restored the dance pavilion that held so many memories from days gone by. The pavilion, built in the 1920s, has a solid maple floor. Cloggers Theresa Silver and Alan Sheppard cut up at Mama T's in the Park, a summertime program of mountain music and dancing sponsored by the Parks and Recreation Department in the restored pavilion. Photograph by Jack Tessier.

True to the tradition of the Scotch-Irish, many of whom populated the western counties, the Asheville Highlanders were in demand for many years to play for parades and convention groups. This 1975 picture shows the Highlanders entertaining at the Grove Park Inn. Notice the variation of tartans worn by the members. With great pride many of the Highlanders trace their ancestors back to the Scotish Highlands and chose the tartans worn by their clan. Photograph courtesy of James H. Coman.

By 1970 American Enka Corporation on the banks of Hominy Creek had become a leading American manufacturer of man-made fiber with over seven thousand employees. During that same period Enka combined with several other industrial plants around the country and Akzona, Incorporated was formed with headquarters in Asheville. Algemene Kunstzijde Unie N.V. of the Netherlands had built American Enka in 1928 on Hominy Creek. The creek was rerouted to circle the 2,200 acres purchased by the plant. BASF Corporation bought American Enka in 1985. Photograph courtesy of James H. Coman.

A flood that caused disaster around the county in February 1977 washed away the Jones Valley Baptist Church in Sandy Mush, leaving only the front entrance and bell tower. The church has been rebuilt in another location. Photograph by David Holt.

Waters from the 1977 flood went through Candler Supermarket with a vengeance, upsetting food cases and ruining the market. Water from Hominy Creek stood as high as three feet. Photograph courtesy of Bill Williamson.

Pisgah View Ranch sprawls on the backside of Mount Pisgah on property that was included in the land grant issued for Uriah Davis 1790. For many years Chester Cogburn served as host for the ranch and entertained guests with his jokes and stories. His wife, Ruby Davis Cogburn, and family still operate the ranch. Photograph courtesy of Ruby Davis Cogburn.

Very near the site of Buncombe county's early Bee Tree settlement, the hills are alive with hazardous waste. Beginning in the 1940s, Oberlikon Corporation, a Swiss company, manufactured explosives and missiles at a site just west of Swannanoa and shipped them around the world. The U.S. government had hoped to buy materials from Oberlikon, but wouldn't because the company was also doing business with Germany. In the 1950s Celonese Corporation used the property to make CS gas and parachute flairs for the Korean conflict. During the Vietnam crisis Northrup made BZ gas. Later it was Cemtronics and now Jet Research and Tandy Corporation are using the site. During this time hazardous waste has been buried or dumped into lagoons protected by levees. Finally, in 1979, at the insistence of a citizens group, the Environmental Protection Agency conducted an investigation. The result is a ruling requiring the last three companies involved to finance a clean-up. This photograph is from the early stages of the development. The Blue Ridge parkway is highly visible in the background. Photograph courtesy of James H. Coman.

The rhododendron of Craggy Bald that bloom in mid-June are a draw for those who drive the Blue Ridge Parkway. The Catawba rhododendron seen here is a large cluster of blossoms, blending from shades of light pink to dark rose. It is usually found high on the mountain balds, different from the Carolina rhododendrons that line the streams of Western North Carolina. In the parlance of mountain people Carolina rhododendron was called "laurel" and what we call laurel was "ivy." When the early explorers and settlers spoke of going through a "laurel hell," they may very well have meant rhododendron. Photograph courtesy of James H. Coman.

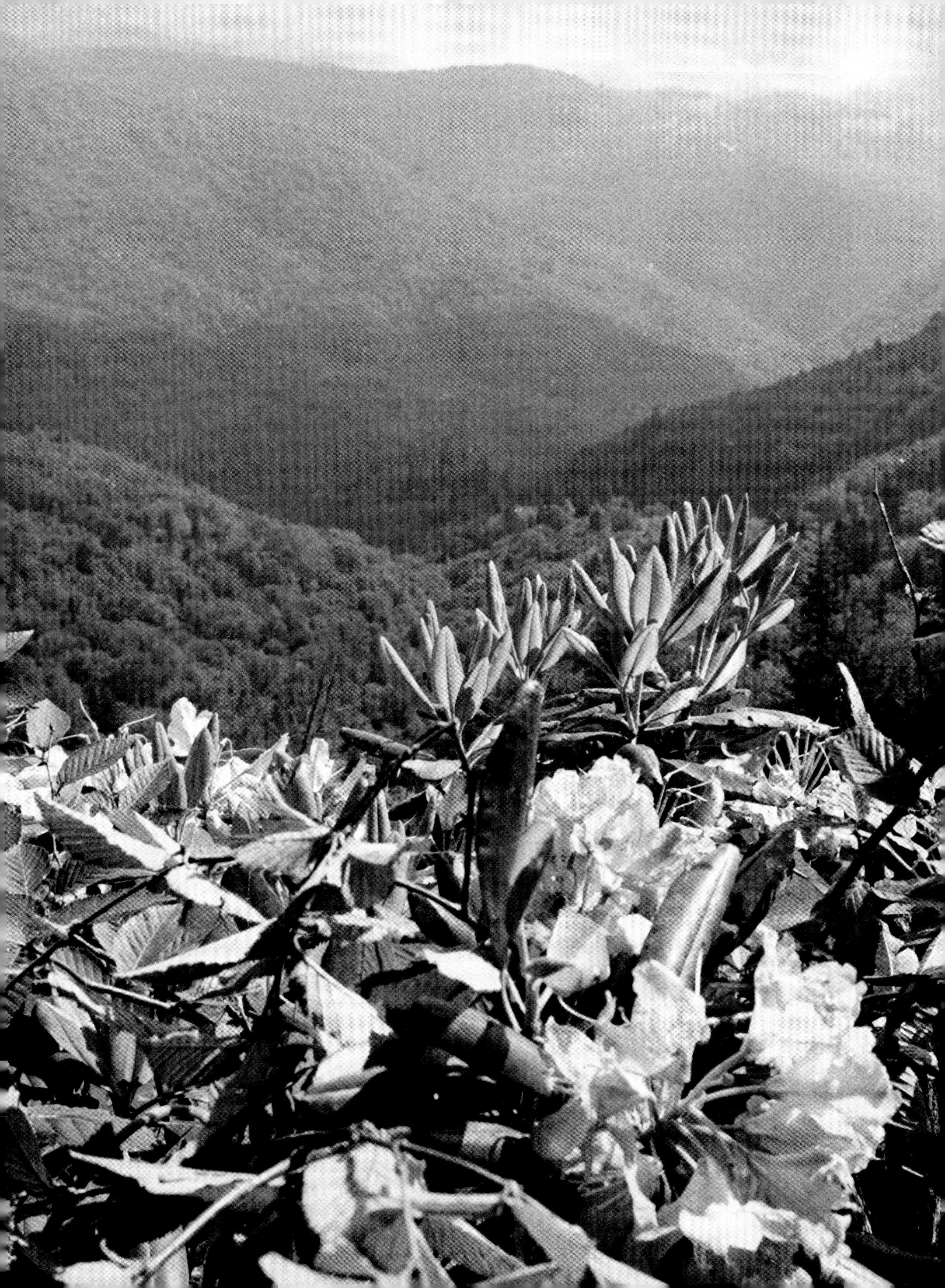

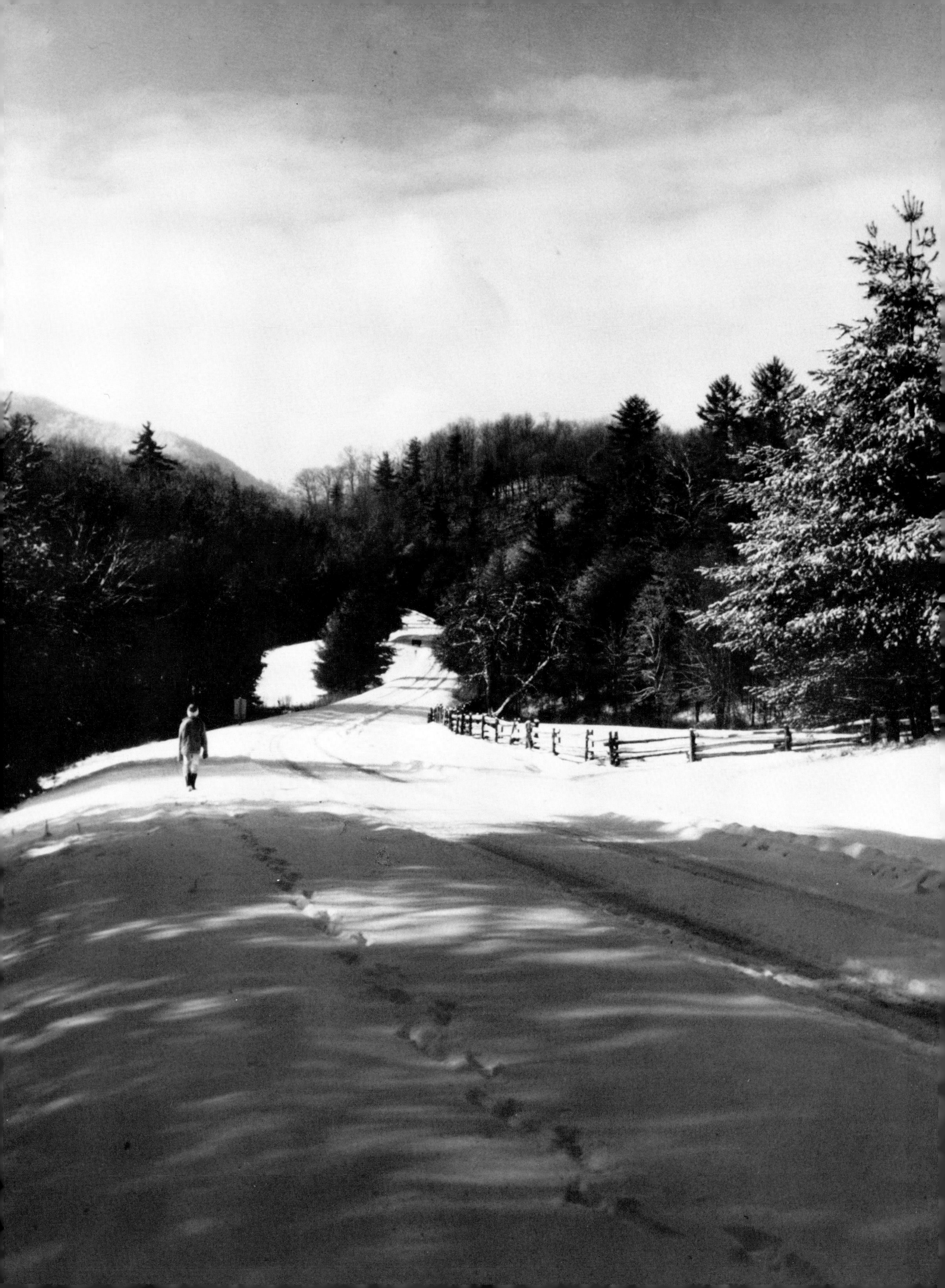

Solving Problems for a Bright Tomorrow

1980 to Today

New jobs and more retirees have swelled county population 8.6 percent from 1980, bringing it to 174,821 in the 1990 census. Industrial jobs, the improvement of county elementary schools, and suburban shopping malls have drawn families to the county and brought on a flurry of housing construction.

With so many men and women entering the work force, farm labor is scarce. About two percent of the residents of Buncombe are employed in farming, forestry, and fishing, though total income from agriculture may go over fifty million dollars.

How to take care of future growth has become the problem. The Water Authority hunts for a new water source, and County Commissioners battle landfill and recycling questions. More space for county offices and what to do about an outmoded jail are also on the docket.

As Buncombe County moves into the third century, a sense of what made her great among the western counties is growing. The strength of the men and women that match the mountains, a moderate climate, the beauty of her surroundings, and a desire to be the best will carry her forward.

When the snow falls on the Blue Ridge Parkway, the barriers go up, the traffic stops, and the mountain road becomes a winter wonderland for hikers and cross-country skiers. Photograph courtesy of James H. Coman.

Preparation for paving on Patton Avenue in 1982 stripped the asphalt away and revealed streetcar tracks still set in old brick. These tracks were laid about 1888 when the street car line that first went down South Main Street was extended onto other streets. Photograph courtesy of Eleanor N. Rice.

Diplomat Richmond Pearson's grand Victorian mansion Richmond Hill was endangered when the Asheville-Buncombe Preservation Society purchased it from the Western North Carolina Baptist Retirement Home. After several years of fund raising, the society engaged Crouch-Mitch House Moving Company of Asheville to place the house on wheels and pull it to a waiting site six hundred feet to the east. The company received a national award for moving the largest structure in the United States during 1984. Estimated weight of the house was one and one half million pounds. In 1887 the Educational Center, Inc., of Greensboro, bought the mansion, directed a two-million-dollar restoration, and reopened Richmond Hill as an inn and conference center. Photograph by Mitzi Tessier.

Ginseng, or "sang" as it was known to the early population of Buncombe County was a cash crop from the time the first settlers began moving into the mountains. It was dug from the woods, along with other medicinal herbs, dried and sold to herb merchants. "Sang" was shipped to Philadelphia and then to China, where there is still a market for it. "Sang" is grown professionally now by men like Fairview farmer Horace Moore. Photograph courtesy of David Holt.

In buildings designed by Richard Morris Hunt for use as dairy barns, the Biltmore Estate is producing fine wines and champagne. Since 1985 visitors to the estate have been able to tour the winery when they visit the Biltmore House. Photograph courtesy of James H. Coman.

No one likes hazardous waste, particularly in the pristine valley of Sandy Mush in northwest Buncombe. When the Department of Energy considered an eastern site for the disposal of hazardous waste in 1986, a large tract of mountain land which included Sandy Mush was discussed. The Sandy Mush Community Club sprang into action, became part of Save the Mountain activists, and arranged a meeting with then Vice President George Bush in Asheville. The man facing Bush on his left is Bill Duckett, president of the club. Others identified are Garrett Smathers, Linda Greene, and Joe Beck. This group stayed active until the DOE suspended a search for an eastern site. Photograph courtesy of Bill Duckett.

Though income from the sale of agriculture products in Buncombe County amounts to over fifty million dollars a year, farms and farmland are still being threatened by "urban sprawl." For that reason the county commission of 1989 voted for a voluntary farmland preservation program ordinance. Under the provisions of the ordinance farmers could form agriculture districts of farms totaling one hundred acres. These districts would then be protected from having to pay for sewer or water lines that crossed their land, unless the land owners hooked on to them. Also, they would be protected from nuisance suits brought by nearby homeowners. Photograph courtesy of James H. Coman.

Amy Reeves of Leicester was only five when she began showing cattle for the 4-H Club. Amy is now a young teenager who recently won a state contest in horticulture. She hopes to be a veterinarian. Amy's father, Kenneth Reeves, is director of the Buncombe County Extension Service. Photograph courtesy of Mabel Duckett.

Valley Springs School on Long Shoals Road in South Buncombe formerly housed the elementary school and high school. More recently the Middle school used these buildings. Spring of 1991 was the last year these buildings were used. Now, high school students attend T. C. Robertson High School and other grades are in new facilities. Photograph courtesy of Amy Smith.

Nationwide attention has been focused on the Center for Creative Retirement at the University of North Carolina at Asheville, so much so that President George Bush named the program his 360th Point of Light. The program has many facets, several of which are intergenerational, as this picture shows. In the university's chemistry department senior research associate Ed Shurts, right, worked with undergraduate research student Rodney Martin to unravel the mysteries of the Massbauer Spectroscopy. Other opportunities available through the center include senior leadership training, off campus reading-discussion groups, Elderhostel, tutoring of elementary and high school students, the College for Seniors, a year-round program for senior advanced study, and participation in national studies on senior interests. In the fall of 1992 the Center will publish the Older Americans Almanac. Retireees in Western North Carolina have made a financial impact on the region, according to UNCA sociologist Dr. Bill Haas. He calculates the total value of weekly expenditures for a group of 814 senior households in the western counties at $14.1 million. Between 1987 and 1989 the average cost of a home purchased by a senior family was $108,884. Photograph by Benjamin Porter.

The Asheville Plant of Burlington Industries, first named Elk Mountain Cotton Mills, then Martel Mills, closed its doors in 1991 after almost ninety years of operation in the textile industry. To the north of the mill is the Metropolitan Sewage Plant. The French Broad River at this point is dammed and electricity is generated by the recent reconstruction of the Weaver Power Dam. Photograph by Malcolm Gamble. Photograph courtesy of Historic Resources Commission.

Said to be one of the oldest cemeteries in Asheville, Newton Cemetery on Biltmore Avenue is undergoing a face-lift under the supervision of the Community Foundation of Western North Carolina. Graves of James McConnell Smith, his family, and other pioneers may be found at Newton. The cemetery and school returned to the trustees in 1988 when the Asheville City Schools decided not to hold classes there. Money gained from sale of the school property to Memorial Mission Hospital is being used to restore the cemetery. Photograph by C. Michael Baker.

As Buncombe County enters the third century, it's well to put together a picture album of a few of the events and people who have gone before. Just as with personal collections, however, the pictures at a certain point turn to color. In these last pages, the evidence of history are present, but Buncombe County today is here, also. This is not the end of the book, but just the beginning.

To the north of Mount Pisgah where Hominy Creek begins, lie two-thousand acres of land that were granted to Uriah Davis in 1790. In the early spring when the dogwood and redbud put on their flowers and the hardwoods are sprouting green the mountain looks massive against the evening sky. Photograph by Jack Tessier.

Kristianna Bartow is dangling in her fingers a medal that will be one hundred years old in 1992. The medal and a special flag were made to commemorate the Centennial of Buncombe County. On one side is engraved, "North Carolina." On the other side are two female figures and the words, "Centennial Anniversary of Buncombe County. Held at Asheville, August 10-11, 1892." Kristianna is a direct descendent of pioneer settler Joseph Rice, who is credited with having killed the last buffalo seen in Buncombe County, at Bulls Gap about 1810. Photograph by Jack Tessier.

Farmers of Western North Carolina gained a new facility for selling produce and fruit with the opening of the state farmers market in 1977. The market provides a retail market where merchants sell craft items, honey, jams, molasses, and produce and a wholesale market where farmers sell in quantity off their trucks. Having a marketplace for the farmers is a tradition as old as Bascombe County. Photograph courtesy of Western North Carolina Farmers Market.

Evangelist Billy Graham and his wife Ruth Graham have dedicated fifteen hundred acres of woodland for a bible training center called The Cove. The property near Azalea east of Asheville is under development. The William F. Chatlos Memorial Chapel, shown here, is complete. Also finished is an administration building and a training center. Cove Camp is open for young people, age nine to eighteen. Photograph courtesy of The Cove.

It's a tiny, insignificant building in a trailer park, but the small library building that Frances Goodrich built in 1895 focuses large in the history of mountain handicrafts. Goodrich and her friend Evangeline Godbold moved to Brittains Cove near Weaverville and taught Sunday School in the library. There, Mrs. William Davis brought a lindsey-woolsey comforter and the paper pattern, or draft. Goodrich became so intrigued with the beauty and simplicity of the handwoven piece that she organized a home industry of women who cold work on some phase of making comforters. She marketed their work in the North and at an Asheville store called Allenstand. The crafts introduced by Goodrich and her group found a ready market around the turn of the century, as international interest in arts and crafts developed. Photograph by Jack Tessier.

A wealth of Art Deco style buildings in Asheville provides plenty of opportunity for students in the painting and decorating class at Asheville Buncombe Technical Community College. The twenty-four-month curriculum prepares graduates for restoration and preservation projects and for working with designers who specialize in faux finishes and wall-coverings. Certificates are awarded by City and Guilds of London. In this photograph the seal of Asheville on the Asheville City Hall is being restored by one of the advanced students. The class, also, has restored the color and gilt in the ceiling of the Buncombe County Court House and redecorated the Smith-McDowell House Museum in the gaudy colors of Victorian America. Encouragement for the course in Asheville came from William Cecil, owner of the Biltmore House, when he was faced with the problem of finding crafts persons in the United States who could maintain the house. Photograph courtesy of Asheville Buncombe Technical Community College.

Will Waldrop was an excellent carpenter. Several evidences of his work can be found in Sandy Mush, some with more ornate woodwork than others. Two small country stores are on Willow Creek Road, just off Bald Creek Road. The smaller store was built by Waldrop soon after he moved to Sandy Mush in the early 1890s. Success in business led him to build the larger, two-story building before the decade had ended. The store, still open as a general store, attracts people from as far away as Spring Creek, Tennessee, over the mountain. Photograph by Jack Tessier.

179

When the Asheville-Buncombe Preservation Society bought the Manor Inn in 1989, the one-hundred year old building seemed destined to feel the weight of the wrecking ball unless a buyer could be found. In the spring of 1991 salvation arrived. The society found a buyer who will convert the Manor into apartments. In the meantime, filmmakers are using it as a set for The Last of the Mohicans. The doorway added to the Tudor-style building is supposed to represent upper New York state in the 1600s. Photograph by Jack Tessier.

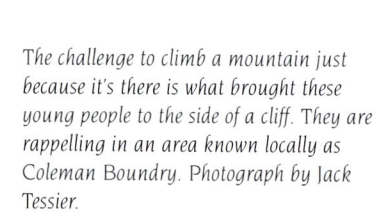

The challenge to climb a mountain just because it's there is what brought these young people to the side of a cliff. They are rappelling in an area known locally as Coleman Boundry. Photograph by Jack Tessier.

Henry Stevens and Ellen (Nelly) Carson moved into a log, dog-trot cabin soon after their marriage in 1868. The cabin was located on land that had belonged to his grandfather, Absalom Dillingham. For almost a hundred years members of the family lived in the cabin. About 1982 the Big Ivy Historical Society bought it and moved it across Dillingham Road to community club property near Barnardsville. They furnished it in the style of the 1880s and have opened it as a house museum. A single pen cabin equipped for the kitchen is believed to be the original cabin in which Henry and Nelly lived. The larger cabin was built later. Photograph by Mitzi Tessier.

International evangelist Billy Graham occasionally finds time to come home to the mountains and relax on his front porch. The Grahams live in Montreat, near Black Mountain. Among his many activities, speaking around the world, writing, teaching, and overseeing the Minneapolis-based Billy Graham Evangelistic Association, Reverend Graham has served as spiritual advisor to several presidents. Photograph courtesy of the Billy Graham Evangelistic Association.

Proof that evidences of history are all around us surfaced again when land for the North Carolina Arboretum was being surveyed. The Arboretum, 424 acres of woodland surrounded by Bent Creek Experimental Forest, is a state facility under development as an education/demonstration center for plant and conservation information. On the grounds, near a curve in Bent Creek, archaeologists discovered a site where an Indian village may have been. Excavation under the supervision of archaeologists Mike Baker and Linda Hall confirmed their theory. In this photograph Baker and Hall are showing their discoveries to George Briggs, director of the arboretum. Dating of post holes, pottery, charcoal, and pieces of bone from a large-hoofed animal, probably elk, have led them to believe the site was inhabited from possibly 200 B.C. to A.D. 1000. Photograph from the United States Forest Service, Department of Agriculture.

In addition to the central branch on Haywood Street in downtown Asheville, the Asheville-Buncombe Library System maintains seven permanent branches and a rolling one. The current bookmobile has been operating since January, 1990. It stays on the road five days a week, carrying books to senior citizen centers and outlying communities in Buncombe County. Photograph courtesy of Pack Memorial Public Library.

Fourth grade students of the city and county schools descend on downtown Asheville each May for a tour of historic sites and a lesson on the history of the city. In 1989 Discovery Day was coordinated with the ceremony to break ground for Pack Place Education, Arts and Science Center, and the children released hundreds of balloons to honor the occasion. Photograph courtesy of Asheville-Buncombe Discovery.

The growth of the county continues and so does the need for new housing. The Reems Creek Golf Club is following the trend toward golf club developments. Rolling mountain land has become an eighteen-hole golf course with homes surrounding its challenging holes. Photograph courtesy of Reems Creek Golf Club.

Sometimes the best way to preserve an old building is to find another use for it. The Reems Creek Milling Company opened in 1914 in this building and operated as a grist mill, making flour and meal until 1950. Today it is a restaurant. The mill wheel is gone, but the workings of the mill are intact. The two-story building was erected on the site of the Reems Creek Woolen Mills, which opened about 1870 under the direction of John Cairns, bought wool from the farmers, and made cloth suitable for men and women's clothing. When the woolen mill was converted to a gristmill, Mrs. George Vanderbilt bought the looms for her industrial school in Biltmore Village. The looms are now housed in the Biltmore Homespun Shop back of the Grove Park Inn. Photograph by Mitzi Tessier.

Galax is a popular plant for Christmas arrangements because the leaves stay bright green and waxlike all winter. For that reason it has always been a money-maker for the "wildcrafters," those who make a living gathering native plants, roots, and herbs. This photograph of the galax was made by Jack Tessier near the Linn Cove Viaduct in Avery County. The viaduct, which goes around Grandfather Mountain, is the last link in the Blue Ridge Parkway, started fifty-two years ago.

When Asheville has a parade, the Shriners come. Members of the Oasis Mountain Dune Buggy Club turned out in the winter of 1991 to welcome home men and women who had served in Operation Desert Storm. A. F. "Tony" Felthaus is driving, with Virgil "Beekus" Bradley as his passenger. Photograph by Mitzi Tessier.

Keeping the integrity of the homesite and the cabin have been the main concerns for the Ralph Mabe family as they restored the Lewis Snelson cabin built about 1840. To the back of the old cabin the Mabes attached a second pen of similar construction. The kitchen adjoins the two. The barn was left intact, and the spring in a grove of trees below the house supplies water. Photograph by Mitzi Tessier.

When George Vanderbilt envisioned his home in the rolling hills south of Asheville, he hired architect Richard Morris Hunt. Together he and Hunt planned a 210-room chateaux, reminiscent of the grand mansions in the Loire Valley of France. Vanderbilt was a collector of fine things and a student of landscaping and agriculture. Landscape architect Frederic Law Olmstead surrounded the home with beauty, a park and formal gardens, but left plenty of area for farming and the development of fine Jersey milk cows. As Vanderbilt's dreams grew, his estate grew. At the time of his death in 1914, he owned 125,000 acres, including Mount Pisgah, and had developed a school of forestry to reclaim damaged woodlands. Photograph courtesy of the Biltmore Estate.

Azalea gardens on the Biltmore Estate were dedicated to Chauncey Delos Beadle in 1940. The gardens were laid out by Frederic L. Olmstead when he did the landscape plan for the estate, but Beadle took special interest in their development and traveled extensively to collect specimens. Beadle served the estate from the early 1890s when he started as nursery supervisor until his death in 1950. At that time he was superintendent of the estate. Photograph courtesy of the Biltmore Estate.

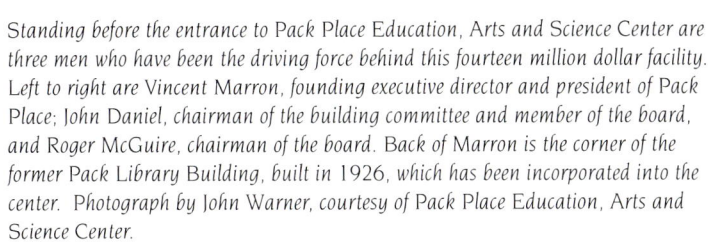

The schedule for the Western North Carolina Agricultural Center has been full year-round since its opening in 1983, with horse shows, rodeos, livestock judging, 4-H events, and auto auctions. In fact, the state facility is so busy there is talk of building another one somewhere in the western counties. Photograph courtesy of the Western North Carolina Agricultural Center.

Standing before the entrance to Pack Place Education, Arts and Science Center are three men who have been the driving force behind this fourteen million dollar facility. Left to right are Vincent Marron, founding executive director and president of Pack Place; John Daniel, chairman of the building committee and member of the board, and Roger McGuire, chairman of the board. Back of Marron is the corner of the former Pack Library Building, built in 1926, which has been incorporated into the center. Photograph by John Warner, courtesy of Pack Place Education, Arts and Science Center.

187

When the sun sets behind the western mountains and the fresh air of a mountain summer evening blows away the heat and problems of the day, settlers of this county called Buncombe know again why they're here. It's more than a hunger for land, wealth, or fame. Those could be garnered better in another place. It even transcends tradition or identity with family. It is, instead, a release, a renewal, a finding of one's self. As Frances Tiernan said when she saw this view in 1875, "This is the land of the sky." Photograph by the Reverend Dr. Robert Tuttle.

Bibliography

Black, David R., ed. *Historical Architectural Resources of Downtown Asheville, North Carolina*. Division of Archives and History, North Carolina Department of Cultural Resources, 1979.

Blackmun, Ora. *Western North Carolina: Its Mountains and Its People to 1880*. Boone, N.C.: Appalachian Consortium Press, 1977.

Blethen, Tyler and Wood, Curtis, Jr. *From Ulster to Carolina: The Migration of the Scotch-Irish to Southwestern North Carolina*. Cullowhee, N.C.: Western Carolina University, 1985.

Caldwell, Wayne T. *Standing on the Promises: A History of Hominy Baptist Church 1812-1987*. Asheville, 1987.

Camp, Cordelia. *Governor Vance: A Life for Young People*. Raleigh: Department of Cultural Resources, 1980.

Diggs, George A. *Historical Facts Concerning Buncombe County Government*. Asheville, 1935.

Dykeman, Wilma. *The French Broad*. 2nd. ed. New York, Chicago, San Francisco: Holt, Rinehart and Winston, 1974.

Ehle, John. *The Road*. New York, Evanston, London: Harper & Row, 1967.

Goodrich, Frances Louisa. *Mountain Homespun*, 1931. 2nd ed. New introduction by Davidson, Jan. Knoxville: University of Tennessee Press, 1989.

Grosscup, Ben S. and Zeigler, Wilbur E. *From the Heart of the Alleghenies of Western North Carolina*. Raleigh, 1883.

Harshaw, Lou. *Asheville: Places of Discovery*. Lakemont, GA: Copple House Books, 1980.

Miller, Leonard. *Education in Buncombe County 1793–1965*. Asheville: Miller Printing Co., 1965.

Osborne, Josephine and Teague, Wanda Peek. *The Tribe of Jacob: a Supplement, 1962–1984*. Weaverville: Bonnie Brae Publications, 1984.

Pickens, Nell. *Dry Ridge*. Asheville: Miller Printing Co., 1962.

Ready, Milton. *Asheville: Land of the Sky*. Northridge, Ca.: Windsor Publications, 1986.

Roberson, Zera Hall. *Public School Education in Buncombe County 1935–1969*. Asheville: Miller Printing Co., 1969.

Sondley, Foster A. *A History of Buncombe County North Carolina*. 2 vols. Asheville: Advocate Printing Co., 1930.

Swaim, Douglas, ed. Articles by Ager, John and Powell, Talmage. *Cabins & Castles: The History of Architecture of Buncombe County, North Carolina*. Asheville: North Carolina Department of Cultural Resources, 1981.

Tessier, Mitzi S. *Asheville: A Pictorial History*. Norfolk: Donning Co./Publishers, 1982.

Government Publications

Buncombe County Agricultural Extension Service. "Buncombe County Agriculture: Food and Fibre". North Carolina Agricultural Extension Service, 1987.

Nesbitt, William A. "History of Early Settlement and Land Use on the Bent Creek Experimental Forest, Buncombe County, North Carolina". Mimeographed. Appalachian Forest Experiment Station, 1941. U.S. Department of Agriculture: Forest Service. "Bent Creek: Research and Demonstration Forest". 1991.

Manuscripts

"Early Churches: In Observance of Reformation Day." Dry Ridge Museum, 1985.

"History of Buncombe County." Mimeographed. Charles E. Newcomb Collection, 1950–56.

"History of Black Mountain, North Carolina." Senior History Class, Black Mountain High School. Mimeographed. 1933.

"History of the Montmorenci Methodist Church." Candler, NC, 1957.

Magazine Articles

Johnston, Pat H. "Pisgah Forest and Nonconnah Pottery." *The Antiques Journal*, May 1977, 12–49.

Stephens, Irby. "Asheville: The Tuberculosis Era." *North Carolina Medical Journal*, September, 1985: 455–463.

Newspapers

Asheville Citizen. 80th Anniversary Edition. March 26, 1950.

Asheville Citizen-Times. 100th Anniversary Edition. January 26, 1969.

Index

A

Abell, Margaret, 131
Abernathy, Irene, 93
Acton United Methodist Church, 142
Ager, John, 54
Akzona, Incorporated, 163
Alba Hotel, 88
Albemarle Inn, 110
Alexander, 65, 73, 137
Alexander, Col. James Mitchell, 30, 49
Alexander, Rachael, 16
Allen, A. W., 14, 117
Allenstand, 66, 178
Allison, Harlie, 60
Ambler, Dr. George, 81
Amboy Road, 157
American Enka Corporation, 112, 146, 155, 163
Archer, Dr. I. J., 117
Arden, 49, 65
Arden House, 49
Arden Park Hotel, 49, 74
Armstrong, E. J., 47
Armstrong, John, 106
Armstrong, Wilbur, 106
Asbury, Bishop Francis, 11, 20, 21
Asbury United Methodist Church, 21, 38
Asheville Area Chamber of Commerce, 124, 161
Asheville Art Museum, 123
Asheville Biltmore College, 62, 125
Asheville Buncombe Technical Community College, 55, 148, 155, 179
Asheville Business College, 113
Asheville Cemetery Company, Incorporated, 135
Asheville City Hall, 124, 139, 179
Asheville City School Board, 147
Asheville Colored Hospital, 146
Asheville Community Wood Yard, 130
Asheville Country Club, 121
Asheville Electric Company, 108
Asheville High School, 155
Asheville Highlanders, 162
Asheville Junction, 69
Asheville Junior Chamber of Commerce, 153
Asheville Library Board, 48
Asheville Recreation Park, 89, 134, 162
Asheville School, 61, 81
Asheville Street Railway Company, 46
Asheville-Buncombe Library System, 182
Asheville-Buncombe Preservation Society, 170, 181
Ashworth, Claude, 93
Ashworth, Elsie, 93
Ashworth, Jason, 82
Ashworth, Nanie, 93
Audubon Lodge, 74
Avery's Creek community, 68
Azalea, 178
Azalea Veterans Hospital, 111

B

BASF, 163
Baird, Bedent, 13
Baird Bottoms, 121
Baird, Gen. Vic, 71
Baird or Lane Iron Works, 40
Baird, Zebulon, 13, 113
Baker, Mabel, 127
Baker, Mike, 181
Bald Creek Road, 179
Ballard, Vasco, 143
Bank Hotel, 49
Bank of Cape Fear, 49
Barnardsville, 37, 181
Barnardsville School, 84, 105
Barnhill, William A., 32, 101, 106
Barrell, Columbus, 120
Bartok, Bela, 119
Bartow, Kristianna, 177
Bass, Minnie, 93
Battery Park Hill, 75
Battery Park Hotel, 78
BB&T Building, 145, 160
Beadle, Chauncey Delos, 186
Beale, Charles Willing, 49
Beale, Mrs. C. W., 49
Bear Creek Ford, 11, 118
Beaucatcher Cut, 89
Beaucatcher Gap, 89
Beaucatcher Mountain, 63, 78, 89, 115, 122

Beaucatcher Tunnel, 89
Beaver Creek, 121
Beaver Lake, 121
Beaver Lake Country Club, 121
Beaverdam, 19, 38
Beaverdam Road, 21, 38
Beck, Joe, 172
Bee Tree, 16, 17, 23, 37, 70, 166
Bee Tree Lake, 122
Bee Tree watershed, 122
Beech, 28, 48, 101, 136
Beech Community Club, 136
Beech Community Fourth of July, 95
Beech Presbyterian Church, 133, 135, 136
Bell Sand Company, 157
Ben Lippen school, 11
Bent Creek, 12, 14, 68, 85, 181
Bent Creek Research and Demonstration Forest, 85, 117, 130, 131, 136, 181
Best, 69
Bethel Methodist Episcopal Church South, 60
Beverly Hills, 115
Big Ivy community, 84
Big Ivy Historical Society, 181
Big Sandy Methodist Episcopal Church South, 82
Biltmore, 65, 129
Biltmore Avenue, 48, 49, 62, 70, 72, 92, 110, 116, 125
Biltmore Building, 145
Biltmore College, 120
Biltmore Estate, 7, 13, 69, 171, 186
Biltmore High School, 125
Biltmore Homespun Shop, 183
Biltmore Hospital, 146
Biltmore House, 76, 87, 119, 121, 171, 179
Biltmore Village, 183
Bingham Academy, 76, 81
Bingham, Col. Robert, 76
Black Mountain, 36, 65, 70, 75, 77, 87, 94, 117, 118, 119, 130, 132
Black Mountain College, 118
Black Mountain High School, 36
Black Mountain Inn, 94
Black Mountain Music Festival, 118
Blackstock, Nehemiah, 37
Blake, Daniel, 41
Blake, Dr. Frederick, 41
Blake House, 41
Blanton, Charles D., 73, 75
Blount, John Gray, 12
Blue Monte, 88
Blue Ridge, 12, 17, 54
Blue Ridge Assembly, 98
Blue Ridge Mountains, 12, 16, 17, 53, 54
Blue Ridge Parkway, 166, 169
Bonniecrest Inn, 74
Bradley, Elsie Martin, 98
Bradley, Virgil "Beekus," 184
Brank, Lucinda, 58
Brank, R. G., 58
Brannon, Mary, 91
Brewton, Dr. Allen, 146
Brick Church School, 82, 120
Briggs, George, 181
Bright, Albert, 93
Britt, J. J., 113
Brittain, Benjamin Stringfield, 17
Brittain, Delilah Stringfield, 17
Brittain, James Stringfield, 17
Brittains Cove, 66, 76, 178
Broby, Hans, 112
Brooks Cove Road, 85
Brooks, Thomas, 71
Brown, Cancel, 98
Brown, Irene, 98
Brown, J. Evans, 89
Brown, Jean, 156
Brown, John, 13
Brown, John Evans, 63
Brown, Lawrence, 84
Brown, Pauline, 98
Brown, Rev. Thomas K., 84
Brown, Roy, 98
Brown, Sewell, 98
Brown, T. K., 75, 94
Brown, Tennie, 98
Brown, W. A. G., 93
Brown's Chapel Missionary Baptist Church, 84
Brush Hill School, 51
BSAF, 163
Buckner, Martha, 143
Buena Vista, 65
Bugg, David N., 156
Bulls Gap, 177
Buncombe Centennial, 69, 73, 177
Buncombe, Col. Edward, 7, 13
Buncombe County Bicentennial Commission, 7
Buncombe County Court House, 17, 35, 66, 123, 124, 125, 145, 179
Buncombe County Court of Pleas, 13, 15, 17, 19

Buncombe County Criminal Court, 69
Buncombe County District Agricultural Fair, 97
Buncombe County Golf Course, 19
Buncombe County Health and Welfare Departments, 159
Buncombe County School Board, 51, 125, 147
Buncombe Hall, 7
Buncombe, Joseph, 7
Buncombe Junior College, 125
Buncombe Riflemen, 69
Buncombe Turnpike, 20, 29, 35, 57, 70
Burgin, John, 127
Burlington Plant, 158, 174
Burnetts, 70
Burton, John, 19
Burton, Kirby, 156
Busby Hall, 74
Buxton, Reverend Jarvis, 38
Bynum, Curtis, 112
Bynum, Mrs. Curtis, 112

C

Calvary Episcopal Church, 112
Camp Rockmont, 118
Candler, 99, 139
Candler Academy, 122
Candler, Coke, 86, 91
Candler High School, 91, 122
Candler, Lucinda, 91
Candler, Miss Lillie, 86
Candler School District, 122
Candler Supermarket, 165
Cane Creek, 17
Cannon, William, 12
Capps, Hubert, 126
Carolina Creamery, 112
Carolina House, 46
Carrier Bridge, 61
Carrier, Edwin George, 61, 157
Carson, Ellen (Nelly), 181
Carson School, 84
Carson Store, 84
Carter, J. E., 143
Carter, Solomon, 36
Case, ___, 12
Case, Arthur, 116
Case, C. O., 116
Case, John F., 116
Cathey, Charlotte, 91
Cathey, Edna, 91
Cathey, Florence, 91
Cathey, George, 91
Cathey, Judge Sam, 71
Cathey, Willa, 127
Catholic Hill, 115
Cecil, William, 179
Center for Creative Retirement, 174
Central Bank and Trust Company, 115, 129
Champion, Callie Allison, 60
Chapman, Robert H., 46
Cherokees, 11, 12, 14, 43
Children's Home, 125
Chiles, Jake, 92
Chiles, Leah Arcouet, 92
Chockley, John, 127
Chockley, Louise, 127
Chockley, Walter, 127
Christ School, 39, 81
Christian Creek, 16
Christmont, 65
Chunn, Samuel, 29, 30, 39
Chunns Cove, 47, 96, 106
Church Street, 39
Church Street Library, 39
City Hall, 59
Civil War, 38, 44, 45, 46, 47, 69, 71
Civilian Conservation Corps, 136
Clarence Barker Memorial, 146
Clark, Agnes, 120
Clark, Bernice, 156
Clark, Carl, 120
Clark, Doyce, 91
Clark, Henrietta, 120
Clark, Hillard, 120
Clark, Homer, 120
Clark, Hoyle, 120
Clark, Nevie, 120
Clark, Sally Hall, 156
Clark, Wilder, 120
Clarke, Lt. James McClure, 141
Clarke, Mrs. Dumont, 141
Clarke, Reverend Dumont, 133, 136 141
Cloister Condominiums, 47
Clyde Savings and Loan Company, 159
Cogburn, Chester, 32, 156, 165
Cogburn, Christine, 153
Cogburn, Ruby Davis, 165
Cole, Dock, 91
Cole, Jo Anne, 156
Coleman Boundry, 180

Coleman, Col. Thad, 54
Coleman, Sara, 95
Coleman, William, 40
College Street, 50, 61, 66, 75, 124
Colvin, James G., 78
Community Foundation of Western North Carolina, 175
Connally, Reverend John Kerr, 55
Connally's Hill, 55
Conway, Robert, 155
Cordelia Camp, 37
Corn Club, 101, 103
Court Plaza, 115
Cove Camp, 178
Coxe, Col. Frank, 75
Craggy Bald, 166
Cragmont Sanitarium, 117
Creasman, Blake, 121
Creasman, William Newton "Kirk," 60
Crockett, Davy, 16
Crouch-Mitch House Moving Company, 170

D

Daniel Boone Camp, 14, 117
Daniel Boone Council, 117
Daniel, John, 187
Daniels, Porter, 127
Daugherty, Garfield, 127
Daugherty, Iddie, 127
Daugherty, Perk, 127
David Miller Junior High School, 125
Davidson, Col. A. T., 66
Davidson, Col. William, 7, 12, 13, 15
Davidson, Dr. Jan, 66, 76
Davidson, Harry, 127
Davidson, James, 12
Davidson, Mrs. Robert, 36
Davidson, Samuel, 16
Davidson, Theodore, 69
Davidson, William, 16, 19
Davidson's Fort, 16
Davis, Mrs. William, 66
Davis, Strobic Hawkins, 98
Davis, Uriah, 165, 177
Davis, William, 178
Deaver, Col. Reuben, 61
Deaver Hotel, 61
DeBord, Kathy, 156
DeBrew, Charles, 91
Democrat, 36
Deweese, Nellie Allison Hughey, 60
Diggs, George, 123
Dill, Harry, 117
Dillingham, Absalom, 181
Dillingham, Harris, 84
Dillingham Road, 181
Dillingham, Walter, 127
Dockery, Mabel, 121
Dodge, William W., Jr., 155
Doe, Mrs. Dora W., 74
Doe, Thomas, 74
Dogged Mountain, 24
Donkel, D. M., 143
Donkel, George, 143
Dorothy Walls Assembly, 117
Dougherty, Maj. John, 98
Drake, Carrie, 121
Drake, Elsie, 121
drovers, 35
Dry Ridge Museum, 9
Dryman, ___, 12
Duckett, Annie Dee, 120
Duckett, Arlious, 44
Duckett, Bill, 172
Duckett, Capt. Wesley, 43
Duckett, Clyde, 151
Duckett, Edward, 44
Duckett, Frankie, 120
Duckett, Fulmer, 120
Duckett, Harriet Louisa, 44
Duckett, Hilda, 120
Duckett, James, 44
Duckett, James Asberry, 44
Duckett, Lassie, 120
Duckett, Margaret, 120
Duckett, Margaret "Peggy" Crawford, 44
Duckett, Margie, 120
Duckett, Maudie, 44
Duckett, Merenda Jane, 44
Duckett, Nora Burress, 44
Duckett, Phyletus, 44
Duckett, Saray An, 44
Duckett, Thelma, 120
Duckett, Troy, 120
Duckett, Will, 82
Duckett, Zene, 120

E

Eagle Hotel, 72
Earley, Clarence, 127

Earley, Juanita, 127
Earley, Boss, 124
Earley's Mountain, 63
Earwood, Mr., 106
East Street, 59
Ebenezer School, 120
Edgemont Road, 119
Edneyville, 11
Educational Center, Inc., 170
Edward Buncombe Chapter of the American Daughters of the Revolution, 49
Ehle, John, 54
Eliada Home for Children, 54
Elk Mountain, 115
Elk Mountain Cotton Mills, 174
Elk Mountain Road, 87
Ellington, Douglas, 115, 124
Ellis, R. Lee, 117

F
Fairview, 65, 83, 124
Fairview Academy, 93
Fairview Collegiate Institute, 93
Fairview Inn, 82
Farm School, 135
Farmer, Henry, 143
Farmer's Federation, 136, 153
Farmers' Market, 178
Fellowship of the Royal League, 117
Felthaus, A. F. "Tony," 184
Fernihurst, 55
First Congregational Church, 117
First National Bank Building, 48
First Presbyterian Church, 39, 135
Flat Creek, 37
Fletcher, Beale, 140
Fletcher, Maria Beale, 140
Florence Stephenson Hall, 62, 146
Fortune, Fletcher, 36
Fox, Johanna, 155
Freeman, Portia, 93
French Broad Avenue, 110
French Broad community, 23
French Broad River, 12, 14, 18, 20, 30, 35, 40, 55, 61, 67, 73, 90, 97, 108, 130

G
Garrison, William, 71
Gashes Creek, 53
Gaston, Ida Sue, 122
Gaston, Percy, 71
George, John, 12
Giles, Gensie, 120
Giles, Gomer, 120
Giles, Manson, 120
Giles, Velda, 120
Gilliam, ____, 93
Gillim, Brig. Gen. Alvan C., 46
Ginseng, 171
Girl Scouts, 156
Glady Fork School, 86
Glass, Lloyd, 60
Glass, Will, 60
Gleltsmann, Dr. J. W., 59, 92
Glenn Bridge Road, 68
Glenn's Creek, 19
Godbold, Evangeline, 76, 178
Goldstein, Robert C., 113
Gombroom, 71
Goodrich, Frances, 66, 76, 178
Gorman, Col. William, 30
Gorman's Bridge, 30
Government Street, 75
Grace Episcopal Church, 89
Graham, Billy, 178, 180
Graham, Ruth, 178
Grassy Branch, 61
Green, Bryan, 127
Green, Fannie, 127
Green, J. M. (Jim), 71
Greene, Linda, 172
Greenville to Asheville Plank Road, 29
Gresham Hotel, 94
Grey Eagle, 75
Groce, T. A., 91
Grove Arcade, 139
Grove, Edwin Wiley, 81, 118
Grove Park Development, 81
Grove Park Inn, 81, 162, 183
Grove Park School, 119
Grovemont, 115, 118
Grovestone quarry, 118
Guastivino, Raphael, 87
Gudger, Adolphus, 19
Gudger, Capt. J. M., Sr., 71
Gudger, Dr. D. M., 60
Gudger, Dr. David, 71
Gudger, Elizabeth Lowry, 36
Gudger, Eva Lane, 36
Gudger, Harry, 91

Gudger, James, 14, 19, 36
Gudger, Judge Owen, 11, 71
Gudger, Mrs. D. M., 60
Gudger, Samuel Bell, 36
Gudger, William, 71
Gudger, William Sr., 19
Gum Springs, 13
Guy, Mrs. Frank, 141

H
Haas, Dr. Bill, 174
Hall, Alton, 91
Hall, Bobby, 111
Hall, Edna, 120
Hall, Elsie, 120
Hall, Helen, 120
Hall, Linda, 181
Hall, Lizzie, 120
Hall, Zera, 122
Hamilton, Susan, 156
Harris, Mrs. M. H., 123
Harris, Sharon, 156
Haw Creek School, 155
Hayes, Martha, 45
Haywood County, 12, 17, 23, 117
Haywood Street, 75, 90; Bridge, 130
Hazel, 65
Head, Millard, 60
Hemphill, J. M., 36
Henderson, Flora, 93
Henderson, Henry, 143
Henderson, Mrs. Henry, 143
Henderson, Rena Lowe, 98
Henderson, Zed, 126
Hendricks, Ollie, 76
Henry, Beth, 142
Henry, Betty Osborne, 142
Henry, Jimmie, 142
Henry, Philip S., 63
Henry, Robert, 17, 61
Henry, William Vance, 142
Henry's Station, 54
Herren, J. R., 84
Hickory Nut Gap, 141
Hicks, Wesley, 71
Hillard Hall, 49
Hipps, Ralph, 91
Historic Resources Commission, 19
Holcombe, Blanche Davis, 35
Holcombe, Glenn, 35
Holcombe, Harriet, 84
Holcombe, John, 84
Holcombe, Julie, 84
Holcombe, Richard Monroe, 35, 84
Holcombe, Theron Augustus, 35
Holcombe's Perennial Seed Company, 35
Hollywood, 115
Hominy, 68
Hominy Baptist Church, 85
Hominy Creek, 11, 12, 36, 165, 177
Hominy station, 83
Hominy Valley, 11, 12, 14, 86
Hood, Reverend Jacob, 60
Hoodenpile, Philip, 30
Hopper, Alvira, 36
Hot Springs (Warm Springs), 58
Howard, Sadie, 91
Howell, Corrlie Lee, 91
Howell, Pat, 91
Hozier, Harry, 11
Hughey, Jim, 71
Hunt, Richard Morris, 50, 69, 171, 185
Hunter, Billy, 71
Hunter, H. F., 93
Hyatt, Mildred, 91
Hyde, Reverend W. M., 136, 140

I
In the Oaks, 119
Inanda, 65
Ingle, Maxine, 140
Ivy Township, 36

J
Jamison, Avery, 91
Jamison, Florence, 127
Jamison, Willie, 127
Jarrett, John, 30
Jarvis, J. C., 36
Jaynes, Clara, 122
Johnston, Avaline Lance, 68
Johnston, Charles Winfield, 68
Johnston, Edith, 68
Johnston, Margaret, 68
Johnston, Meta, 68
Johnston, Samuel, 68
Johnston, Thomas, 71
Johnston, Walter, 68
Jones, Bob, 93
Jones, Francis Josiah, 24

Jones, Horace, 24
Jones, Kate, 93
Jones, Laura M., 110
Jones, Mac, 93
Jones, Pink, 85
Jones Valley Baptist Church, 164
Jupiter, 65

K
Kenilworth, 92, 115
Kenilworth Inn, 69
Kennickell, Virginia, 82
Kennickell, Herman, 82
Killian, Daniel, 21, 38
Killian, Josie, 21
Killian, Julia, 21
Killian, Wally, 38
Kirk, Gen. George W., 46

L
Lake Eden, 118
Lake Louise, 40
Lake Marjorie, 67
Lake Shore Drive, 50
Lake Susan, 88, 100
Lake Tomahawk, 132
Lakeshore Avenue, 67
Lakeview Park, 115, 121
Lance, ____, 12
Lance, Doris, 127
Lance, Everett, 127
Lance, Macy, 127
Lance, Manning, 85
Lane, Nora, 120
Langren Hotel, 145
Leatherwood, Glenda, 156
Ledbetter, Everett, 83
Ledford, Mary, 91
Lee, Col. Stephen, 47
Lee, Gen. Robert E., 46
Lee, Mary Robinson, 127
Leicester, 65, 98
Lester, Dr. P. C., 49
Lexington Ave. (Water St.), 148
Liberty school, 127
Limestone area, 49
Little Salisbury, 53
Littrell, Mr. and Mrs., 104
Llewellyn, Dara, 156
Long, Kathryn, 156
Long, Mary, 156
Long, Sara, 156
Long Shoals ford, 18
Long Shoals Road, 18, 173
Long, Thomas, 82
Lord, W. H., 84
Lords Acre Project, 133
Lotspeich, Bascom, 40
Lotspeich, Louise, 40
Love, Robert, 19
Lowe, Nora, 98
Lowe, Plummen, 98
Lowry, Col. James, 19
Lowry, David, 19
Lyda, Fred, 93
Lynch, Edna, 93
Lytle, Albert, 71
Lytle, James (Potts), 127

M
Mabe, Ralph, 185
MacFee, Bill, 12
Macon County, 155
Malonee, George, 91
Malta Window Center, 113
Malvern Hills, 115
Mama T's in the Park, 162
Manley and Bell, 94
Manor Inn, 181
Marron, Vincent, 187
Martel Mills, 174
Martin, Brigadier General James G., 46
Martin, Davie, 98
Martin, Rodney, 174
Masonic and Temperance High School, 50
Matthews, Johnny, 111
Matthews, Mussendine, 15
McAfee, Grace, 93
McAfee, Reverend D. Cleland, 140
McCall, Kay, 156
McClure, Elspeth, 141
McClure, James G. K., 141
McCormick Field, 111, 114
McDowell, Gen. Joseph, 15
McDowell, Maj. William Wallace, 69, 110
McDowell Street, 115
McElreath, Martin, 127
McGuire, Roger, 187
Medical Building, 75
Memorial Mission Hospital, 62, 146, 175

Meredith, Jack, 60
Meredith, Jim, 60
Meredith Lela Allison, 60
Merrill, Carl, 93
Merrimon Avenue, 89
Metropolitan Sewage Plant, 174
Miami Mountain, 75
Milburn and Heister, 125
Mill Creek, 54
Miller, George Douglas, 87
Miller, Judy, 156
Miller, Leonard P., 60
Miller, Lillian, 93
Mills River Academy, 65
Mineral Springs Hotel, 74
Minnie Bass, 93
Mitchell, Reverend Dr. Elisha, 126
Mitchum, Robert, 146
Monte Vista Road, 35, 85, 127
Montford, 129
Montmorenci United Methodist Church, 62
Montmorencie (sic) Methodist Episcopal Church South, 62
Montreat, 65, 77, 100, 180
Montreat College, 77
Montreat Inn, 88
Moore, Capt. William Hamilton, 11, 12, 16, 60
Moore, Charles, 60
Moore General Hospital, 139
Moore, Horace, 171
Moore, Judge Walter E., 78
Morgan, B. L., 62
Morgan, Evelyn, 122
Morgan, Wayne, 91
Morriss, Elizabeth C., 110
Morristown, 12, 13
Mount Mitchell State Park, 126
Mount Pisgah, 165, 177, 185
Mountain Dance and Folk Festival, 161
Mountain Lily, 57
Mountain Meadows Inn, 87
Mountain Park Hotel, 58
Mountain Retreat Association, 77
Mt. Carmel Baptist Church, 137
Mud Cut, 54

N
National Casket Plant, 113
Nesbitt, William A., 49
New Asheville Speedway, 157
Newfound, 11, 45
Newington, 41
Newton Cemetery, 175
Newton, Reverend George, 17, 50
Newton School, 17, 38, 116
Nolen, Dr. John, 121
Normal and Collegiate Institute, 62, 113, 125
North Asheville, 129
North Carolina Arboretum, 181
North Carolina State Militia, 11, 43, 68
North Fork, 71, 113
North Fork watershed, 89
North Main Street, 46
Northwestern Bank Building, 160

O
Oak Grove Farm, 106
Oakley Baptist Church, 161
Oakley High School, 120
Oasis Mountain Dune Buggy Club, 184
Oates Field, 111
Old Farm School Road, 51
Old Fort, 16, 54
Old Leicester Highway, 137
Olmstead, Frederic Law, 185, 186
Osborne, Joseph, 38
Osborne, Virginia, 140
Oteen Hospital, 139
Owen airfield, 157
Owen, Dr. J. E., 126
Owen, Jamie, 96

P
Pack, George Willis, 48, 66, 78, 123, 124
Pack Memorial Public Library, 9, 66, 123, 137, 160, 187
Pack, Mrs. George Willis, 66
Pack Place Education, Arts and Science Center, 123, 182, 187
Pack Square, 66, 71, 123, 129, 160
Palmer, David, 82
Palmer, Jeper, 82
Parham, "Chubb," 161
Parham, Milburn, 127
Parham, "Red," 161
Parker, Capt. William, 79
Parker, James M., 58
Parker, Mathilda, 58

191

Patton Avenue, 75, 112, 170
Patton, Col. T. W., 46, 89
Patton, Elizabeth (Polly), 16
Patton, James, 29, 38, 39
Patton, Robert, 155
Payne, Malinda, 63
Payne's Chapel, 63
Peabody Educational Fund, 51
Peach Knob, 87
Pearson, E. W., 97, 107
Pearson Park, 97, 107
Pearson, Richmond, 67, 108, 170
Pease, Mrs. Louis M., 62
Pease, Reverend Louis M., 62
Peebles, Sharon, 156
Pelton, H. W., 94
Penland, Clara, 122
Penland, Dave, 95, 104,
Penland, F. A., 48, 105, 143
Penland, Helen, 91
Penland, Jake, 140
Penland, Nancy Stevens, 45
Penland, Reverend Alfred M., 48, 143
Penland, Sallie, 91
Penland, Sara Lewis, 95
Penland Stone Pottery, 99
Penland, William, 12
Penley, Dilla Ray, 60
Penley, Howard, 127
Peppertree Resorts, Limited, 63
Pete Luther Road, 127
Petit, Terrie, 127
Piney Grove Presbyterian Church, 37
Pisgah Highway, 62, 68
Pisgah National Forest, 81, 117, 126
Pisgah Pottery, 107
Pisgah View Ranch, 156, 165
Pitillo, Riley, 71
Pitillo, Rollie, 93
Plateau Studios, 113, 121
Pleasant Grove Church, 58
Pleasant Grove Road, 58
Plemmons, Erskine, 98
Plemmons, Howard, 98
Plemmons, Hyleman, 98
Plemmons, James, 98
Plemmons, Levi, 45
Plemmons, Mae, 98
Plemmons, Mark, 98
Plemmons, Reverend Erskine, 137
Plonk, Laura, 119
Plonk, Lillian L., 119
Plonk School of Creative Arts, 119
Point Tunnel, 54
Pondoppidan, Hans, 112
Pondoppidan, Hendrik, 112
Porter, E. M., 17
Porter, William S. (O'Henry), 95, 135
Powell, Margaret, 91
Powell, Mary, 91
Pressley, Carl, 127
Pressley, Margaret, 127
Price, Jonathon, 12
Pritchard Hall, 88
Pritchard Park, 75, 132
Pritchard, Sen. Jeter, 81
Pullian, Marlow F., 126
Public Square, 15, 35, 39, 43, 46, 49, 55, 59, 67, 72, 76, 78, 89, 124
Pyatt, Joseph B., 41

R
Radisson Hotel, 159
Ragsdale, Gabriel, 12
Raines, Martha, 36
Ramsey, D. Hiden, 155
Ravenscroft School, 38
Ray, Charles Sherman, 61
Ray, Charlotte Ida, 61
Ray, Ernest, 87
Ray, James Albert, 61
Ray, Jesse Alexander, 60
Ray, John, 61
Ray, Lona Belle, 61
Ray, Luther, 87
Ray, Martin, 61, 111
Ray, Martin L., 111
Ray, Marvin, 61
Ray, Sophronia Creasman, 61
Ray, William Festus, 61
Ray, William Riley, 60
Reagan, Dr. James Americus, 51
Reed, Edna, 93
Reems Creek, 17, 23, 24, 40, 48, 51, 79
Reems Creek Golf Club, 183
Reems Creek Milling Company, 183
Reems Creek Presbyterian Church, 50
Reems Creek Road, 79, 155

192

Reems Creek Woolen Mills, 183
Reeves, Amy, 173
Reeves, Kenneth, 173
Reynolds, Abraham, 12, 14
Reynolds, Alonzo Carlton, 120
Reynolds, Dr. Carl V., 119
Reynolds, Mary Leazer, 14
Rhea, Chloris Penland, 143
Rhea, James S., 101
Rhea, Leonard, 101, 155
Rhodes, Linda, 156
Rhymer, Deana, 127
Rice, J. W., 62
Rice, Joseph H., 51, 177
Rice, Nancy, 153
Rice, Reverend William Francis, 87, 89
Riceville, 61, 76
Riceville Presbyterian Church, 76
Riceville Road, 60, 87
Riceville School, 100
Richmond Hill, 67, 76, 108, 170
Ridgecrest, 54, 65, 88
River Ridge Factory Outlet, 53
Riverside Cemetery, 39, 71, 95, 135, 158
Riverside Park, 108, 111
Riverside Road, 113
Roberson, Cash, 91
Roberson, Milton, 86, 139
Roberson, Thomas Crawford, 103, 147
Robert E. Lee Hall, 98
Robeson, A. C., 82
Robinson, Alexander, 39
Robinson, Clyde, 127
Robinson, Lowell, 127
Rogers, ___, 12
Rosscragan Inn, 74
Rough and Ready Guards, 71
Royal Giants Baseball Team, 107, 111
Royal Pines, 40
Runnels, Abraham, 85
Rutherford, Brigade General Griffith, 11
Rutherford ford, 18
Rutherford, James, 12
Rutherford, Pansy, 12, 91
Ryman, C. P., 107

S
Sale, Fred, 121
Sale, J. D. Murphy, 121
Salem, 11
Sams, Capt. Edmund, 30
Sand Hill, 11
Sand Hill Academy, 60
Sand Hill High School, 139
Sandy Mush, 19, 24, 43, 44, 63, 82, 120, 164, 172, 179
Sandy Mush School, 110
Sandy Mush United Methodist Church, 82
Sapp, James T., 130
Sawyer community, 24
Sawyer, Gregg, 155
Sawyer, James, 84
Sawyer, Nancy, 84
Schenck, Carl, 81
Schoenberger, Mr., 38
Scott, Bain, 120
Scott, Bertie, 120
Scott, Dorothy, 120
Scott, Mrs. David, 143
Seeley's Castle, 125
Sellers, Harry, 91
Sevier, John, 11
Sheppard, Alan, 162
Sheraton Hotel, 159
Shope, Kelly, 87
Shuford, Bonnie, 93
Shurts, Ed, 174
Silver, Theresa, 162
Silverline Plastics, 113
Singleton, John, 141
Sisters of Mercy, 110
Skyland, 116
Slab College, 58
Sluder, Ed, 137
Smart, Laura, 93
Smart, Mattie, 93
Smathers, Garrett, 172
Smathers, John C., 57
Smith, Bedent, 71
Smith Bridge, 30, 58
Smith, James McConnell, 30, 35, 71, 175
Smith, Richard Sharp, 69, 72, 78, 89
Smith-McDowell House, 9, 179
Snelson, Faraday, 98
Snelson, Lewis, 185
Solomon, Carter, 36
Sondley, Dr. Foster A., 7, 13, 39, 40, 55, 137
South Main Street, 48, 49, 72, 170
Southern Highland Handicraft Guild, 9, 66
Southern Highlands Research Center, 9

Southern Improvement Company, 58
Southside Avenue, 111
Spivey, ___, 12
Spruce Street, 124
St. Joseph's Hospital, 110
St. Joseph's Sanitarium, 92, 110
St. Lawrence Catholic Church, 87
St. Luke Episcopal Church, 96
Stafford, Eller E., 113
Stafford, Exum Clement, 113
Stephen Lee School, 38, 98
Stephens, Dr. Irby, 92
Stephens, Walter B., 107
Stephens-Lee High School, 115
Stepp, G. W., 75
Stepp, John Meyers, 67, 71
Stepp, Joseph, 71
Stepp, William, 36
Stevens, A. E., 94
Stevens, Alfred, 45
Stevens, David M., 45
Stevens, Dr. J. Mitchell, 45
Stevens, Francis, 45
Stevens, Henry, 181
Stevens, Jesse, 45
Stevens, Merritt, 45
Stevens, Nancy, 45
Stevens, Robert, 45
Stevens, Thomas N., 45
Strawther, 82
streetcars, 129, 132
Strother, John, 12
Struan, 39
Sugar Creek, 24
Sunset Mountain, 81, 129
Sunset View, 74
Swain, Caroline Lane, 19
Swain, David Lowry, 19
Swain, George, 19, 29, 40
Swannanoa, 17, 18, 23, 63, 65, 67, 118, 130, 139
Swannanoa Gap, 11, 43, 88
Swannanoa Hotel, 72
Swannanoa River, 12, 13, 16, 19, 30, 47, 61, 70, 84, 89, 97
Swannanoa school, 84
Swannanoa tunnel, 53, 54

T
T. C. Roberson High School, 125, 173
Tabernacle Meeting House, 36
Tan Yard Branch, 12
Tarbell, J. H., 78
Taylor, Congressman Roy A., 147
Taylor, Margarite, 91
Tennessee-North Carolina border, 12, 15
Terrell's Station, 88
Terry, Franklin Silas, 119
Terry, Lillian Emerson, 119
The Citizens Committee for Better Schools, 147
Thirtieth Division (Old Hickory), 97, 112
Thomas' Legion, 73
Thomas Wolfe House, 159
Thompson's Knob, 12
Thrall, Dr. J. B., 117
Thrash, A. P., 127
Thrash, Augustus Buckingham, 35
Thrash, Hattie, 35
Thrash, John Jr., 35
Thrash, Lucinda Yountz, 35
Tiernan, Frances, 188
tobacco, 43, 149, 150, 151, 153
Tourists (baseball team), 114
Town of Victoria, 70
Turkey Creek, 11, 14, 19, 36, 45
Turkey Creek Baptist Church, 98
Turnpike Company, 29
Turnpike Hotel, 57
Tweed, Theron, 142

U
Union Academy, 17
Union Hill School, 17
University of North Carolina at Asheville, 9, 174

V
Valkyrie, 112
Valley Museum, 9
Valley Springs School, 173
Vance, Brig. Gen. Robert Brank, 15, 69, 73
Vance, Celia, 17
Vance, Col. David, 7, 13, 15, 17, 155
Vance homestead, 155
Vance Monument, 66
Vance, Mrs. Z. B., 71
Vance, Pricilla Brank, 15
Vance, Sen. and Gov. Zebulon Baird, 15, 37, 54, 71, 73, 135, 155
Vanceville on Reems Creek, 15
Vanderbilt, George, 55, 68, 69, 70, 72, 76, 85, 87, 185

Vanderbilt, Mrs. George, 183
Vanderbilt, Mrs. William, 76
Vaughn, Esse, 98
Vehorn, Julia, 93
Victoria Hospital, 62, 146
Victoria Road, 70
Von Ruck, Dr. Karl, 59

W
Waldrop, Will E., 82, 179
Walker, Felix, 9
Walton, Alf, 71
Warren, Cindy, 32
Warren, Henry, 32
Warsaw, 40
Watauga or Bear Creek Trail, 11
Watauga settlement, 11
Watkins, Jean, 156
Weatherford, Dr. W. D., 98
Weaver, Agnes, 86
Weaver, Caroline, 86
Weaver, Elizabeth Biffle, 79
Weaver, Elizabeth Siler, 79, 86
Weaver, Ethan Douglas, 103
Weaver, Glen, 86
Weaver, Hattie Culbreath, 86
Weaver, Jacob, 79, 86
Weaver, Jesse Richardson, 86
Weaver, John, 79
Weaver, Julia Coulter, 86
Weaver, Lucius, 86
Weaver, Lucy, 86
Weaver, Martha Webb, 84
Weaver, Mary, 51
Weaver, Minnie, 86
Weaver, Pearl, 86
Weaver Power Dam, 174
Weaver, Robert, 86
Weaverville, 51, 65, 76, 79, 95, 105, 129
Weaverville Brass Band, 79
Weaverville College, 50, 51
Webb, Stacy Young, 36
Webb, Walter, 98
West Asheville, 129, 130
Westall, Baechus, 71
Western North Carolina Agricultural Center, 187
Western North Carolina Baptist Retirement Home, 170
Western North Carolina Railroad, 54, 70, 88
Western North Carolina Sanitarium, 134
Western Turnpike, 35, 57
Wetmore, Reverend Thomas, 39
Whitaker, George, 71
White, J. J., 71
White, George, 71
White, Sam R., 105
Whiteside, Dorothy, 91
Whiteside, Margaret, 91
Whitside, Betty, 122
Whitson, Max, 134
Whittemore, Paul, 155
William F. Chatlos Memorial Chapel, 178
Williams, Ella Lyda, 93
Williams, Ben, 83
Williams, Charity, 91
Williams, Debbie, 91
Williams, Guy, 71
Williams, Mallie, 93
Williams, Robert, 71
Willow Creek Road, 179
Wilson, Maj. James W., 54
Wilson, Tom, 126
Wilson, Julia, 93
Winyah Sanitarium, 59
Wolfe, Thomas, 134, 135
Woodfin, 113
Woodfin House, 159
Woodfin, N. A., 113
Woodson, Matthew, 37
Worley Cove, 44

Y
YMI Band, 72
Young, Jasper, 36
Young, Linda, 156
Young Men's Christian Association, 159
Young Mens Institute, 72
Young, P. M. B., 73

Z
Zealandia, 63, 89
Zimmerman, Lena, 153